The Play's the Thing:
Teachers' Roles in Children's Play, 2nd Ed.
ELIZABETH JONES & GRETCHEN REYNOLDS

Twelve Best Practices for Early Childhood Education:
Integrating Reggio and Other Inspired Approaches
ANN LEWIN-BENHAM

Big Science for Growing Minds: Constructivist
Classrooms for Young Thinkers
JACQUELINE GRENNON BROOKS

What If All the Kids Are White? Anti-Bias Multicultural
Education with Young Children and Families, 2nd Ed.
LOUISE DERMAN-SPARKS & PATRICIA G. RAMSEY

Seen and Heard:
Children's Rights in Early Childhood Education
ELLEN LYNN HALL & JENNIFER KOFKIN RUDKIN

Young Investigators: The Project Approach in the
Early Years, 2nd Ed.
JUDY HARRIS HELM & LILIAN G. KATZ

Supporting Boys' Learning: Strategies for Teacher
Practice, PreK–Grade 3
BARBARA SPRUNG, MERLE FROSCHL, & NANCY GROPPER

Young English Language Learners: Current Research and
Emerging Directions for Practice and Policy
EUGENE E. GARCÍA & ELLEN C. FREDE, EDS.

Connecting Emergent Curriculum and Standards in the
Early Childhood Classroom: Strengthening Content and
Teacher Practice
SYDNEY L. SCHWARTZ & SHERRY M. COPELAND

Infants and Toddlers at Work: Using Reggio-Inspired
Materials to Support Brain Development
ANN LEWIN-BENHAM

The View from the Little Chair in the Corner: Improving
Teacher Practice and Early Childhood Learning (Wisdom
from an Experienced Classroom Observer)
CINDY RZASA BESS

Culture and Child Development in Early Childhood
Programs: Practices for Quality Education and Care
CAROLLEE HOWES

The Early Intervention Guidebook for Families and
Professionals: Partnering for Success
BONNIE KEILTY

The Story in the Picture:
Inquiry and Artmaking with Young Children
CHRISTINE MULCAHEY

Educating and Caring for Very Young Children:
The Infant/Toddler Curriculum, 2nd Ed.
DORIS BERGEN, REBECCA REID, & LOUIS TORELLI

Beginning School: U.S. Policies in International Perspective
RICHARD M. CLIFFORD & GISELE M. CRAWFORD, EDS.

Emergent Curriculum in the Primary Classroom:
Interpreting the Reggio Emilia Approach in Schools
CAROL ANNE WIEN, ED.

Enthusiastic and Engaged Learners: Approaches to
Learning in the Early Childhood Classroom
MARILOU HYSON

Powerful Children: Understanding How to Teach and
Learn Using the Reggio Approach
ANN LEWIN-BENHAM

The Early Care and Education Teaching Workforce at
the Fulcrum: An Agenda for Reform
SHARON LYNN KAGAN, KRISTIE KAUERZ, &
KATE TARRANT

Windows on Learning:
Documenting Young Children's Work, 2nd Ed.
JUDY HARRIS HELM, SALLEE BENEKE, & KATHY STEINHEIMER

Ready or Not: Leadership Choices in Early Care
and Education
STACIE G. GOFFIN & VALORA WASHINGTON

Supervision in Early Childhood Education:
A Developmental Perspective, 3rd Ed.
JOSEPH J. CARUSO WITH M. TEMPLE FAWCETT

Guiding Children's Behavior:
Developmental Discipline in the Classroom
EILEEN S. FLICKER & JANET ANDRON HOFFMAN

The War Play Dilemma: What Every Parent and Teacher
Needs to Know, 2nd Ed.
DIANE E. LEVIN & NANCY CARLSSON-PAIGE

Possible Schools: The Reggio Approach to
Urban Education
ANN LEWIN-BENHAM

Everyday Goodbyes: Starting School and Early Care—
A Guide to the Separation Process
NANCY BALABAN

Playing to Get Smart
ELIZABETH JONES & RENATTA M. COOPER

How to Work with Standards in the Early
Childhood Classroom
CAROL SEEFELDT

In the Spirit of the Studio:
Learning from the Atelier of Reggio Emilia
LELLA GANDINI, LYNN T. HILL, LOUISE BOYD CADWELL, &
CHARLES SCHWALL, EDS.

Understanding Assessment and Evaluation in Early
Childhood Education, 2nd Ed.
DOMINIC F. GULLO

Negotiating Standards in the Primary Classroom:
The Teacher's Dilemma
CAROL ANNE WIEN

(continued)

The Play's the Thing

Teachers' Roles in Children's Play

SECOND EDITION

Elizabeth Jones
Gretchen Reynolds

Foreword to the First Edition
by Elizabeth Prescott

Foreword to the Second Edition
*by Kathy Hirsh-Pasek and
Roberta Michnick Golinkoff*

TEACHERS COLLEGE PRESS

TEACHERS COLLEGE | COLUMBIA UNIVERSITY
NEW YORK AND LONDON

Published by Teachers College Press, 1234 Amsterdam Avenue, New York, NY
10027

Library of Congress Cataloging-in-Publication Data

Jones, Elizabeth, 1930–
    The play's the thing : teachers' roles in children's play / Elizabeth Jones,
    Gretchen Reynolds ; foreword to the first edition by Elizabeth Prescott. – 2nd ed.
        p. cm. – (Early childhood education series)
    Includes bibliographical references and index.
    ISBN 978-0-8077-5241-8 (pbk. : alk. paper)
        1. Play–United States. 2. Education, Preschool–United States. 3. Teaching.
    I. Reynolds, Gretchen. II. Title.
    LB1140.35.P55J66 2011
    372.210973–dc23   2011016851

ISBN 978-0-8077-5241-8 (paper)

Printed on acid-free paper
Manufactured in the United States of America

18 17 16 15   8 7 6 5 4 3

Contents

Foreword
to the First Edition

Are you disappointed in your ability to promote play, uneasy about the play that does occur, frustrated by your ineffectiveness in responding to play, or exasperated at the low value others attach to it? If you answer "Yes" to any of these questions, this is the book for you. The authors are skillful observers of play, and chapter by chapter they show aspects of play that only those who have watched long and carefully can describe.

My friend Ruth Pearce talks about play as "a bubble of illusion." I have always liked this phrase because it captures the way in which play comes and goes. It can be so brief that it is scarcely noticed before it disappears, or it can be sturdy and complex, with other bubbles attached to it. And since it is pretend, once it vanishes ordinary reality takes its place.

To view play as a bubble also describes the empty space within the bubble where the player as creator places the drama. Within this bubble those things that are forbidden or hopeless in the real world can be pretended. Young children pretend at being adults or at being so powerful that even adults must do their bidding. As the creator of these invented plots, a child experiences personal power. With luck there are also friends to share in these fantasies. It is the wish for both the play and the friendship to continue that makes children willing to give up absolute power and work at compromise.

This empty space also gives the player time to find connections between personal experience and perceptions and the outside world with its rules, expectations, and conventions. Within the bubble of play, the player can tinker with these outside constraints and in the tinkering find ways to keep feelings of initiative and uniqueness intact. Thus logic and motivation become aligned to face together the task of mastering the tools of the culture that schooling will demand. The stories in this book will remind you time and again of the profoundly inventive ways in which children work to make these connections, and since play is self-chosen you will see how children reveal much about themselves.

In my mind play is intimately concerned with boundaries. How do we know certain behaviors are "play"? How do we redefine a situation to turn it into play? These distinctions can be difficult for the mentally ill or for those stepping into a foreign culture. Adults who cannot enter into a playful context often create misery for themselves and others. To play requires great flexibility in thinking, an ability to shift context and to add new ideas. These skills, which will be useful across an entire life cycle, do not come without practice.

When children were reared by mothers who were not employed outside the home, there was scant reason to pay attention to play. It occurred without much planning and was welcomed by adults who could then attend to their own concerns. The typical home was stocked not only with toys, but with a variety of loose parts. There were often older and younger children to introduce novelty, and there were private spaces where children could play without interruption. Adults, though busy with other concerns, were available to be watched or questioned, or to settle conflicts. At lunch or during other routines of care, the play of the morning could be discussed. Thus, the roles described in this book occurred in many homes naturally and without reflection. The behaviors of both parents and children were so embedded in the setting that they became invisible and hence unimportant. Today, as more and more childhood time is spent in a group setting, it has become essential to recreate an experience that once occurred naturally, and to offer this experience to children who in the past did not have supports for play. In order to do this the ecology of play and the role of the adult in fostering it must be examined.

The one thing that I like best about this book is that, for me, it describes the knowledge that is required to foster play and to use it as a solid foundation on which to build learning. As these stories unfold, you will see the possibilities for adults to behave in ways that keep the bubble of play from popping prematurely. To do this often requires that the adult create safe boundaries, both visible, in setting up the environment, and invisible, in using adult logic to create transformations and to attach meaning. I suggest that the chapter titles outline a job description that communicates the high levels of professional skill required of those who work with young children. Perhaps this book tells even more about professional development than about play.

—Elizabeth Prescott

Foreword
to the Second Edition

Clap your hands. Clap them so hard that you join millions of children, scientists, and teachers who feel the fairy dust of educational reform. If we clap loud enough maybe, just maybe, the pages of this book will come alive in classrooms all over the world and adults will see the physicist in the child who builds forts from living room couches and the literary genius that develops within a 5-year-old King Arthur who navigates history from the kitchen table.

Play has become a four-letter word in a culture driven by fear and global competition. On March 23, 2011, *Time Magazine* wrote of a mother suing her child's preschool because "the school proved to be not a school at all, but just one big playroom." More telling was writer Bonnie Rochman's headline for that article which sat on the horns of a false dichotomy: "In Preschool, What Matters More: Education or Play?" (2011). It is precisely this kind of debate that has devalued play and playful learning in our schools. David Elkind (2008a) writes that children have lost 8 hours of play per week in the last 2 decades and a 2009 report from the Alliance for Childhood finds that a sample of kindergarten classrooms in New York and Los Angeles have little time for child-driven activities. Indeed, much of that discretionary time has been replaced with test preparation (Miller & Almon, 2009).

Faced with a persistent achievement gap between lower- and middle-class students and with the empirical realization that early education could narrow that gap, it is little wonder that educators and policymakers are building stronger preschool curricula. The data are clear. Numerous scientific studies affirm that academic and social experiences in the preschool years are associated with stronger school readiness and later school outcomes in language and mathematics (Campbell, Pungello, Miller-Johnson, Burchinal, & Ramey, 2001; Campbell & Ramey, 1995; Campbell, Ramey, Pungello, Sparling, & Miller-Johnson, 2002; Reynolds, Ou, & Topitzes, 2004; Schweinhart, 2004; Weikart, 1998; Zigler, Singer, & Bishop-Josef, 2004). Further, a large survey of six longitudinal data sets from Britain and the United States examined precursors for school readiness (Duncan et al., 2007). Using meta-analyses across thousands of children, researchers concluded that mathematics achievement, emergent literacy scores, and attention skills were the best predictors of later academic success. These results held for children from low and high socioeconomic niches and equally for boys and girls. Thus, researchers are zeroing in on exactly the kinds of curricular goals that will align preschool education with later primary school subjects.

Yet, our science also teaches us that strong curricular goals can be met within playful pedagogies. In *A Mandate for Playful Learning in Preschool* (Hirsh-Pasek, Golinkoff, Berk, & Singer, 2009), we review much of this research that supports the claim that children who learn in playful ways either match or outperform those who learn through direct instruction. And more recent findings underscore this message. Han, Moore, Vukelich and Buell (in press) find that playful learning enhances vocabulary development in preschoolers compared to more didactic practices. Alfieri, Brooks, Aldrich, and Tenenbaum (2010) review 164 studies comparing discovery-based versus direct instruction approaches to learning and find that the discovery approaches trump the kind of learning that emerges in more didactic pedagogies. Finally, research from our own laboratory suggests that children are better at learning and retaining their knowledge of geometric shapes like squares and triangles when they participate in activities that are playful (Fisher, Hirsh-Pasek, Newcombe, & Golinkoff, 2011).

Importantly, this new wave of interest in playful learning, guided play, and discovery learning is signaling a change from the past and a more nuanced approach to the debate. Jones and Reynolds invite teachers to reflect on six possibilities for facilitating children's play competence. Intentional teaching involves making choices and stepping in to support play while respecting the child's agenda is not easy decision-making. Play is children's first language for making meaning of the world. Preschool and kindergarten teachers who care about learning cannot short-change children's time for play in favor of inappropriate academics. Teachers who are *stage managers* set the props for learning, *mediators* help students navigate the social and academic waters, *players* model the rich possibilities in play, and *scribes* document the learning in activities like block play.

Playful learning or guided play sits midway between free play (which is also important) and direct instruction. This is not to say that we should drop all direct instruction. Direct instruction has some benefits for learning things like multiplication tables. Indeed, recent and forthcoming research suggests that children will learn what they are taught. A review of findings from two major longitudinal studies (Early et al., 2005) suggests that students in direct instruction outperform those in free play in both math and reading. Our own research corroborates this finding, suggesting that children learn shapes better in direct instruction than in free play with the same shapes.

The powerful news, however, is that when children engage in playful learning or guided play, they do *even better* than they do in direct instruction, mastering not only simple shapes like triangles, but also more complicated ones like hexagons (Fisher, Hirsh-Pasek, Golinkoff, Berk, & Singer, 2010). And children taught with guided play actually remember the features that define the shapes so that they recognize novel instances—like triangles with smaller angles. Playful learning offers educators a plan for creating fun and engaging pedagogies that support rich curricula (Singer, Golinkoff, & Hirsh-Pasek, 2006). It also offers a vision of how to help children discover (e.g., problem-solving, attention) ways of learning to learn (Li-Grining, Votruba-Drzal, Madonado-Carreno, & Haas, 2010). And this book offers magnificent descriptions and evidence-based examples of how teachers can pave this new road and create a climate for *learning via play*.

It is becoming increasingly clear that the "teacher as director" model will have to give way to the metaphors that dominate this book. If our children are to be prepared for school and equipped with 21st-century skills for learning, they will need to learn more than a list of memorized facts. Rather, they will need to be master what we (Hirsh-Pasek, Golinkoff, Berk, & Singer, 2009) call the 6Cs: Collaboration, Communication, Content, Critical thinking, Creative innovation, and Confidence. Importantly, *content* is one of the skills, but not the only one, required for success in school and in the workplace. *Collaboration* is critical today so that children can learn to work in teams to solve problems and to build communities of understanding. *Communication* encompasses more than just *form*; it includes taking the listener's perspective, regardless of cultural differences, mastering rhetoric, writing, listening, and crafting an argument. *Content* includes the learning of math and reading but also social studies, the sciences, and the arts. As we are told that knowledge is doubling every 2.5 years, simple memorization of the ever-changing "facts" will ultimately be a diminishing quality without c*ritical thinking* or a way to navigate the knowledge. *Creative innovation* allows us to surmount what *Newsweek* dubbed the "creativity crisis" (Bronson & Merryman, 2010) as we link seemingly disparate facts, to envision the next YouTube, and to innovate for the problems of tomorrow. And *confidence* enables children to test new ideas and to take bold but calculated risks.

The 6Cs allow us to imagine a school fashioned for our time rather than a school for the agricultural or industrial age. The 6Cs allow us to imagine a school in which children work together and communicate about higher-order goals that use content skills (geometry for plane design, stories about great pilots) rather than one that focuses on content as an end in itself.

It is time to embrace educational reform—not by patching the old system—but by envisioning a new system of education geared to the outcomes we must achieve in our era. Playful learning offers a metaphor for the types of teaching and learning that will guide us—if only adults, policymakers, and educators can see play through this new lens. As Vivian Paley (1986b) once wrote, "'Birthday' is a curriculum in itself" (p. 126). In birthday scripts children write invitations, count the number of guests, and even do fractions when they divide the cake so that each friend gets a piece.

If we clap our hands hard enough, this message might be heard by the educational establishment and we will create a future where it is not about play *or* education, but rather about playful learning *as* education.

—Kathy Hirsh-Pasek, Ph.D.
Roberta Michnick Golinkoff, Ph.D.

Acknowledgments

During many years' involvement with programs for young children, we have been participants in and observers of a variety of adult interactions with children at play. For several years, as members of a resource support team, we worked with preschool staff in programs sponsored by the Pasadena Unified School District and Pacific Oaks College and Children's School, under the auspices of a public-private Partnership Project supported by the Ford Foundation. We enjoyed the opportunity for sustained observation and reflection, and for fruitful dialogue with teaching staff. We appreciate the contributions everyone made to our thinking and to our collection of stories of children at play.

We want to acknowledge teachers and staff members in the Partnership Project at that time who would recognize some of our stories: Beni Campbell, Jackie Cotton, Erin Sumner, Jackie McMurray, Connie Wortham, Suzanne Duarte Jones, Kathy Reisig, and Caridad Bonilla. In addition, we include observations made by members of our learning community, a network of like-minded teacher researchers who received and contributed to our project newsletter. We are grateful to Pasadena teachers Theresa Barrios and Georgina Villarino, Madison Preschool; Sandra Rangel and staff member Irma Stone, Jefferson Preschool; and Sue Bush and Joyce Mortara, Willard Children's Center; as well as to Linda Torgerson, Juneau Cooperative Preschool, Juneau, Alaska; Gaye Gronlund, Buckeye School District, Redding, California; Anne Solomon, Rocklin School District, California; Joan Newcomb, The Little School, Bellevue, Washington; Wanda Magiera, San Jose, California; and Jamie Solow, observer in project preschools.

In this second edition of our book, we have added several new stories, with our thanks to the teachers, staff, and children at the Ottawa Inuit Children's Centre and the Early Learning Centre, Algonquin College, Ottawa.

We want to emphasize that the views expressed throughout the book are our own; they do not represent the Partnership Project or our subsequent work with other early childhood professionals. Keep in mind that where a "visitor" or "observer" appears in a story, that's one of us.

Introduction

Three-year-olds Rachel and Katy are playing in the kitchen with Mona, a teacher. Two dolls, swaddled tightly in small blankets, have been put down in straw baskets for sleep. Rachel is vigorously stirring the imaginary contents of a saucepan with a wooden spoon. Sitting beside Rachel at the table, Mona folds doll clothes, and one by one, Katy places them in a basket on a nearby shelf.

Putting two cans on the table, Mona offers, "I have some corn and mixed beans for your soup." Rachel smiles and scoops from the cans to add the contents to her saucepan.

Mona picks up a doll. Katy looks closely in her face and asks, "Dollie, do you like this dress? Yes, you do!"

"Shall I hold her while you dress her?" asks Mona. Katy puts the doll's arms in the sleeves and turns her over to do up the snaps.

Rachel lifts the other doll and cradles it in her arms. She begins feeding soup to the doll.

Mona asks, "Baby must be hungry. Is she asking for more?"

"Yeah, she's real hungry," laughs Rachel, pushing another spoonful at the doll. Then she holds the doll upright, patting its back. She smiles and says, "Good baby."

"Oh, nice hug!" Mona exclaims.

What's going on here? Play—by children and their teacher.

This is the first of the many stories about play that we'll be telling in this book—stories that come from our experience. Both to offer continuity to readers and to maintain the privacy of the players, we tell most of the stories as if they happened at either of two composite settings that have no real-life counterpart: Live Oak Child Development Center and Second Street School, both of which are described below.

SETTINGS

Live Oak Child Development Center is located on a community college campus and serves as a laboratory for early childhood education students. Its half-day preschool combines 3- and 4-year-olds; it is taught by several mentor teachers and varying small numbers of students in practice teaching assignments. Its full-day child care program divides the younger and older children for part of the day, but they have free choice together, indoors and out. Its teaching staff is also complemented by students, who have opportunities to plan and lead small-group activities in addition to setting up and maintaining the play environment.

Live Oak's families are culturally, racially, and socioeconomically diverse. Fees vary on a sliding scale determined by family income. Parents may be students, college staff and faculty, and residents or workers in the neighborhood. The home languages of the families vary from year to year and may include Mandarin, Arabic, Spanish, Hindi, and English, among others.

Second Street School is a large public elementary school whose early childhood program includes a child care center and two Head Start classrooms. The child care center has two classes, one of 3-year-olds and one of 4-year-olds. The Head Start is a half-day program for families meeting the income limit; a handful of children stay all day, joining friends in child care for the afternoons. Several teachers are bilingual, alternatively pairing sentences spoken in English and Spanish. When they can, parents volunteer time to help in the classroom or on a trip.

The other programs occasionally named in this book were actual programs with varying structures and populations.

WHY PLAY?

As preschool educators we have our roots in the developmental approaches of Bank Street and Pacific Oaks, two colleges with children's schools whose early childhood traditions predate the impact of Piaget's theory of cognitive development. We taught kindergarten and the primary grades to enrich our preschool experiences, and along the way we became caught up in the new ideas and purposes influencing early childhood education since the 1960s.

Cognitive interpretations of developmental theory, such as the developmental-interaction approach (Franklin & Biber, 1977), emphasize play—autonomous choice of activity—as the primary mode in which young children construct their understanding of the world. This emphasis on play differs significantly from that of cultural transmission theorists (described in DeVries & Kohlberg, 1990; Franklin & Biber, 1977), who regard play as respite from direct instruction, the appropriate mode of teaching. The latter view, based in behaviorist psychology, still dominates kindergarten and primary education (Miller & Almon, 2009). In programs modeled on behaviorism, preparation for 1st grade is the objective, and teachers are to help children overcome deficits. Play has no place in school (Bereiter & Engelmann, 1966).

The developmental psychology of John Dewey inspired Jean Piaget when he joined the Rousseau Institute in Geneva at the end of the first World War. Interested in children's changing patterns of thinking, Piaget observed their spontaneous play and encounters with materials, and he listened to their ideas about how things work. Piaget's theory of children's cognitive development from infancy through late adolescence describes four distinct, hierarchical stages. It describes consistencies in children's ways of approaching materials, their talk about play, their perceptions when they encounter natural phenomena, and causal interferences they draw. The theory was unprecedented in developmental psychology, with its claim that biology and maturation alone do not explain cognitive development. The process that gives rise to knowledge—constructivism—is a child's experimentation or playfulness with materials and reflection on the effects of her actions. In Piaget's words, *To Understand Is to Invent* (1973), knowledge is a reorganization of one's thinking, an accommodation the mind makes resulting in a different perspective, a paradigm shift, and new ways of interacting with the world. In refreshing contrast to the empty vessel image of a child's mind, Eleanor Duckworth (2007), observing "the having of wonderful ideas," describes knowledge construction as a "creative intellectual act"

> whether it is an infant who for the first time makes the connection between seeing things and reaching for them, or Kevin who had the idea of putting straws in order of their length, or a musician who invents a harmonic sequence, or an astronomer who develops a new theory of the creation of the universe. In each case, new connections are being made among things already mastered. (p. 14)

Constructivism, as we have come to understand it, is a powerful rationale for the essential role of play in both cognitive and moral development. It supplements our long-standing awareness of the role of play in socioemotional development and enables us to be more articulate in our advocacy for play. It has supported the extension of advocacy for play—both child-guided and teacher-guided play—into kindergarten and primary education (Bredekamp & Copple, 2009; Epstein, 2009; Fromberg, 2002; Kamii, 1985; Katz & Chard, 2000; Van Hoorn, Nourot, Scales, & Alward, 2011; Wasserman, 2000).

Effective teaching practices in early childhood are developmentally appropriate; they are known to match a child's intellectual, social, and emotional levels of development. Play is the best preparation for school success; early academics impose expectations that result in stress and passivity toward learning (Bredekamp, 2004; Elkind, 2008b). Publication of *Developmentally Appropriate Practice in Early Childhood Programs* (Bredekamp, 1987;

Bredekamp & Copple, 2009) generated broad consensus on the previously vague concept of developmentally appropriate pedagogy. Traditional methods—direct instruction—were easy for teachers, who had plenty of first-hand experience. Developmentally appropriate practice was more difficult; it begins with an understanding of real children in a dynamic environment, not with prescribed curriculum (Wien, 1994).

Vygotsky's (1978) theory of social constructivism inspired a shift in early childhood education theory that places a teacher in an active role as co-player and co-investigator with children during their play and work.

> We feel that the teacher must be involved within the child's exploring procedure, if the teacher wants to understand how to be the organizaer and provoker of occasions, on the one hand, and the co-actor in discoveries, on the other. And our expectations of the child must be very flexible and varied. (Tiziana Filippini, quoted in Edwards, Gandini, & Forman, 1998, p. 181)

The teacher is a resource to children. Also, he designs situations and interventions to scaffold a child's learning, structuring comfortable guidance to match what the child already knows and can do and to encourage her to practice a challenging task with assistance.

Piaget (1962) saw few benefits in pretend play. He regarded it as a sign of cognitive immaturity—a young child's egocentric mind invents and manipulates symbols that have no interface with reality. Not so, according to social constructivism theory and Vygotsky. Self-directed imaginative play itself is the scaffold that mediates young children's learning and is the primary source of development. "In play the child always behaves beyond his average age, above his daily behavior; in play it is as though he were a head taller than himself" (Vygotsky, 1978, p. 102). How so? The structure of social imaginary play (based on real themes or fantasy) is generated by the players as they assume roles, engage in verbal dialogue, and substitute non-replica objects and actions to communicate meaning (Hirsh-Pasek, Golinkoff, Berk, & Singer, 2009; Reynolds & Jones, 1997). Play is intrinsically motivating, and children voluntarily relinquish impulsive behaviors and immediate gratification to align their actions to the unfolding script. In play, "children are active agents who reflect on and coordinate their own thoughts, rather than merely absorbing those of others" (Berk, 2006, p. 627). Make-believe play, drama, and storytelling support practice in emotional self-regulation, teaching children to read contexts and align their actions in response (Leong & Bodrova, 2009; Paley, 2004; Reynolds & Jones, 1997). In self-directed play young children practice empathy—learning sensitivity to one another's emotions and intentions.

Three-year-olds Gloria and Danny are side by side at the table with a winding wooden train track, train cars, and environmental accessories—mountains, road signs, and bridges. Danny focuses on steering his nine-car-long train around a curve, his voice making train-engine sounds. Gloria reaches across the track in front of Danny's train for a vehicle, and Danny protests loudly, "Stop it, Gloria! My train goes there!" Gloria resists, prolonging her stretch across the track. Danny wails unhappily, "Gloria!" Without speaking, Gloria arches her back, her body forming a bridge. Danny steers the train under Gloria's body-tunnel, bringing it out the other side. Both children are laughing, and the play continues.

TEACHER ROLES

The teacher roles described in this book reflect both our theoretical views of what is desirable and our practical experience with what is possible. Working with teachers in the field, we have found that some roles are more readily accepted than others. In this sample of preschool programs, the role of *stage manager* is the most familiar to all the teachers; without exception, the indoor environments are beautifully provisioned for play. When we began the Partnership Project, the outdoor environments varied greatly in quality. The idea of outdoor stage management came as no great novelty, however, and teachers have generally been enthusiastic about expanding their definition of this role.

Teacher as *planner* is another familiar role, although planning for play is less familiar than planning for directed group activities. In our work with teachers, we have continually observed, and communicated to them about, children's sociodramatic play and language, in order to emphasize the value we place on these behaviors in the developmental sequence. Some teachers, especially those inclined to be playful themselves, have increasingly explored the process of planning for play. A number have responded to the idea of providing for literacy as a playscript.

The role of teacher as *scribe*, although a new idea to most of the project participants, has also been greeted with interest. In nearly every classroom adults are writing down children's words and displaying them on classroom walls. Teachers seem to like being "people who write down children's words."

Teacher as *teller*, a role not on our recommended list, is a traditional role clung to by many adults who work with children. When telling becomes part of mediation or of adult play with children, it typically interrupts play. Teacher as *mediator*–someone who helps children find their own solutions rather than imposing an adult solution–appears to be a relatively unfamiliar role, though we have seen many examples of its skillful use by a limited number of teachers.

We keep thinking about the role of teacher as *player*. It is one that both of us, teaching preschool, have moved into naturally, and so our first inclination is to assume that others should, too. As observers, however, we have seen a range of teacher involvement with children at play—some supportive and genuinely playful, some intrusive. We have observed teachers who regularly interact with children at play but fail to support the integrity of the play. Their comments and questions come from their preconceived lesson plans; typically, such questions serve to interrupt the play unless children are able to ignore them.

Most lesson plans identify learning objectives that are dependent on teaching, not on children's spontaneous learning through play. Yet Kamii's (2000) studies of children "reinventing" arithmetic through their play with appropriate materials demonstrate the ways in which learning takes place without direct teaching. Kamii has also described how anxious primary teachers are likely to become if they are not teaching mathematics facts.

Similarly, some teachers become anxious if they are not teaching names of shapes and colors and letter names, even though these properties appear repeatedly in the play materials in a well-provisioned environment and will be spontaneously used as logical categories by playing children. When we encourage teachers to plan for children's learning through play, we some-times encounter resistance. Trust in children as learners is even less easily acquired than trust in oneself as teacher, it appears.

For this reason we continue to look for ways to emphasize the crucial roles of *assessor* and *communicator*. In these roles teachers become able to con-vince themselves, as well as others, that the children really are learning as they play.

This book begins in Chapter 1 with the ideas about play that we have constructed in order to remind ourselves, and others, of the importance of children's play. The first three sections have few stories and no conversa-tions; "'and what is the use of a book,' thought Alice, 'without pictures or conversations?'" (Carroll, 1979/1899, p. 1). You will, however, encounter a conversation in the section on "Master Players," and from then on through-out our book, they'll start to come "thick and fast," in Carroll's words. Chil-dren's play is full of pictures and conversations. We invite readers to share some of those we've observed and listened to.

CHAPTER 1

Understanding and Supporting Children's Play

To become a master player is the height of developmental achievement for children ages 3 to 5. Master players are skilled at representing their experiences symbolically in self-initiated improvisational drama. Sometimes alone, sometimes in collaboration with others, they play out their fantasies and the events of their daily lives. Through pretend play young children consolidate their understanding of the world, their language, and their social skills. The skillful teacher of young children is one who makes such play possible and helps children keep getting better at it.

Many people working with young children, however, have quite a different view of what teachers do: Teachers teach. They sit children in circles, lead finger plays, and talk about the calendar. They tell children the rules for using the slide and for avoiding collisions with the tricycles. When we watch children playing "school," they play stern teachers who give information, enforce discipline, and issue directives. In the school game as played by both children and teachers, there appears to be a consensus that when teachers talk, children learn. How else will they learn right and wrong? How else will they learn colors and shapes and numbers and letters?

Developmental theory, which has had little influence in education beyond early childhood, is quite clear on this point. In Piaget's (1973) words: "the use of active methods . . . give broad scope to the spontaneous research of the child or adolescent and require that every new truth to be learn be rediscovered or at least reconstructed by the student, and not simply imparted to him" (pp. 15–16). Young children learn not by being told but by constructing knowledge through actions with objects in the physical world and interactions with other children—and the way they do this is by playing. "The playing adult steps sideward into another reality; the playing child advances forward to new stages of mastery" (Erikson, 1950, p. 222).

STAGES OF PLAY

The play of 3- to 5-year-olds is different from the play of children before age 3, as well as from that of primary-age children. Developmentally appropriate practice (National Association for the Education of Young Children [NAEYC], 2009) in early childhood programs implies practitioners making decisions that match age-related characteristics of development and learning. It also implies responsiveness to individual and cultural differences, assuring that environments, materials, experiences, and interactions are relevant, meaningful, and respectful. Sustained opportunities for self-chosen play provide the most effective way of responding to these differences.

Erik Erikson and Jean Piaget have offered complementary theories of stages of children's development. Table 1.1, in which we consider the development of play and representation, summarizes their theories and serves as an outline for this chapter. With this framework established, we move on to look at the content of play—its scripts—and its mastery by children. The chapter concludes with the teacher's question, "But what do I do while they're playing?" which introduces the teachers' roles that this book is all about.

Under Three: Exploration

The child under age 3, says Erikson (1950), faces the challenges of developing, first, trust—the ability to connect—and then autonomy—the ability to separate. Piaget (Peterson & Felton-Collins, 1986) describes this as the sensorimotor stage, when knowing is physical. Neuroscience research affirms that newborns' brains are shaped by sensory and movement experiences. Programs can do much more to stimulate infants! Babies need unrestricted movement—fingers, arms, legs, in clothes that allow freedom—and an array of interesting materials, such as papers and fabrics to touch, hold, crinkle, and fold, and colorful balls to bounce, roll, and capture (Lewin-Benham, 2010).

For mobile toddlers and 2-year-olds, the developmental theme is *exploration* of the world through physical action and through the beginnings of oral language. Kept safe by watchful adults, the competent toddler is a vigorous explorer of and with her own body and what it can do, of other people and their reactions, and of the world of interesting things all around. She pokes and dumps and pulls, tastes and smells and strokes whatever she encounters, increasingly adding verbal commentary in order to communicate with others and to reflect her own experiences.

The thoughtful caregiver for the very young provides an environment rich in sensorimotor experiences to be explored (Stallibrass, 1989), mediates to provide safety while teaching problem-solving and respect for differences (Gonzalez-Mena & Stonehouse, 2008), uses language suited to the child's

TABLE 1.1. A Summary of Developmental Stages

	Age		
	0–2	3–5	6–8
Primary Learning Activity	Exploration	Sociodramatic play	Investigation
Focus of Learning	Physical world: direct knowing	Experienced world: in images and stories	Experienced world: classified
Modes of Representation	Body language (gesture); developing oral language	Body language; spontaneous oral language; imaging with materials; dramatic play	Body language; spontaneous oral language; structured oral language; imaging with materials; dramatic play; structured dramatization; developing literacy
Adult Contribution to Representation	Models body language and simple oral language	Models oral language; makes provision for play and imaging; models simple literacy	Models and structures oral language; makes provision for play and imaging; structures dramatization; models and structures literacy
Piaget Stages	Sensorimotor	Preoperational	Concrete-operational
Erikson Stages	Trust and autonomy	Initiative	Industry

understanding, and responds appreciatively to the beginnings of pretend play. She is, above all, a giver of care, of emotional and physical comfort and warmth in relationship.

Three to Five: Play

From ages 3 to 5, says Piaget, the child's mental activity is "preoperational." Knowing becomes more than sensory, but its logic is constructed by the child for himself, in modes quite different from adult logic. Knowing requires spontaneous action, which takes the form of *play*: the self-initiated re-creation of one's experiences in order to understand (assimilate) them. Erikson describes the developmental task of this stage as the achievement of initiative—the capacity to choose and plan and accomplish for oneself without being immobilized by anxiety.

For both Erikson and Piaget, the developmental task in preschool is *mastery of play*, most particularly constructive, dramatic, and sociodramatic play. It is at this age that the young child, involved in experiencing, becomes a competent representer of experience. Human society and human thought are built on the achievement of *representation,* which makes possible both looking back and looking ahead, rather than just living in the moment; and communication removed in both place and time, rather than only face-to-face. The exploration of the toddler is direct encounter, not representation. But the dramatic play of 3-, 4-, 5-, and 6-year-olds is increasingly sophisticated representation of real and imagined experiences and ideas.

In their representation, preschoolers make use of spontaneous oral language, which they have typically mastered in its basics and which they continue to refine and expand. They supplement speech with body language, using their whole selves to enact the dramas that comprise their worlds. In their action, they are storytellers—creators of narratives that, as they play together, become the shared mythology of the community of children. Their stories are enriched by props and costumes, just as the stories of older actors are. Like any preliterate people, they rely on, and continue to create, an oral tradition shared in face-to-face encounters. Their knowing is, in Donaldson's (1978) word, *embedded* in their doing.

Simultaneously, given the availability of cultural tools for the purpose, they are creators of images. Opportunities to make one's mark in the world with pencils and pens, crayons and markers, paints and chalk, fabrics, and hands shaping clay and play dough enable the child to explore, and eventually use in intentional representation, the construction of visual imagery, which in all cultural traditions complements the spoken word. These "soft" media are balanced by the hardness of wood scraps and tools and glue, blocks and Legos, and natural and found stuff (Topal & Gandini, 1999), all of which impose the discipline of learning to fit them together and achieving balance, but can then be used for the child's own re-creation of the buildings, roads, machines, and natural phenomena surrounding her.

Young children represent their thinking, ideas, and experiences through pretend play and through complementary experiences with construction and art tools of every variety. Representation is a tool for thinking. To represent is to revisit, revise, and re-create. Children learning to draw also *draw to learn* (Forman, 1996). The construction of shared imagery by children makes their community of experience visible.

The teacher of preschool and kindergarten is concerned with children's mastery of play, oral language, and imagery. She provides a play environment rich in possibility with time and space for children to be alone and together. To make their togetherness most productive, she mediates and models empathy and fairness, the use of language for problem-solving, and the divergent thinking essential to negotiation with others who are different from oneself. Through props and ideas shared in conversation and storytelling, photos and documentation, she challenges children to complicate their playscripts and expand their repertoire of dramatic themes. She models appropriately complex oral language and integrates opportunities for literacy and numeracy as more abstract modes of representation.

Developmentally, the thinking of 4- and 5-year-olds is preoperational, learning by doing. If kindergarten is children's first organized group experience, it serves as a benign orientation to the people, place, and materials of the school, and a chance to learn to play together, be considerate of one's peers, and recognize the teacher's authority. Although many children now enter kindergarten with several years' group experience, their modes of knowing and doing are appropriately those of 5-year-olds. Kindergarten, for a competent preschooler, is the opportunity to demonstrate and enjoy mastery of play, to experience the peak of success in doing what one does best in response to the cognitive challenge that play offers children (Smilansky, 1968). In play, children learn to plan (Reynolds, 1988). In contrast, "academic" kindergartens reflect a deficiency model rather than a competence model, demanding premature practice of what one *doesn't* know how to do.

> A kindergarten without substantial playtime puts everyone at a disadvantage, for play is still the primary reality for its members. Play contains the only set of circumstances children understand from beginning to end. "I can do this well," the kindergartners seem to say. "I can be this effectively. I understand what is happening to me and to the other children." (Paley, 2009, p. 61)

Six to Eight: Investigation

Mastery of age-related tasks is the best possible preparation for children about to enter school. Dyson (1989) describes in detail the ways in which the oral language and drawing skills that primary children have already attained help them in their efforts to practice story writing. A primary classroom in which at writing time children are free to talk and draw, as well as write, enables them to utilize all the skills gained in play as they move into the tasks of the stage Erikson identified as *industry*. Piaget used "concrete operational" to describe the mental capacities of children ages 6, 7, and 8; they are rational thinkers who are able to use logic (as much of the Western world defines it) in the understanding of their hands-on experiences. They are able to generalize beyond the direct evidence of their senses, though not to forgo such evidence and learn through words alone.

In the primary years, children become "serious players," in Wasserman's (2000) phrase. Katz and Chard (2000) and Wasserman have clearly described the ways in which developmentally appropriate curriculum in primary schools engages children's minds by challenging them to think critically and reflectively about the *investigations* they undertake, both in child-initiated activities and in their action and interaction as serious players at play-based learning activities that are teacher-guided. Children able as concrete-operational thinkers are ready for the group-conversational conscious reflection on their play that Wasserman calls "debriefing." Unlike preoperational children, they are intentional learners, capable of product–as well as process–orientation, which in the world of school is a marker of achievement. They can be guided to set goals for themselves and evaluate their learning, and to design how they will improve or build on this learning at the next opportunity.

Primary teachers provide a balance between "breathing out"–self-chosen activity in which children continue to consolidate their understandings as they did in preschool–and "breathing in"–teacher-designed challenges that enable children to "uncover" concepts in the curriculum (Ashton-Warner, 1963; Hawkins, 2002). Teachers guide group conversation about shared experiences and help children learn to ask good questions (Forman, 1989). Further, they guide meaningful practice in the use of literacy and numeracy–the basic abstract modes in which people represent experience. In the primary years, children are ready to begin acquiring the disembedded (Donaldson, 1978), decontextualized (Snow, 1983) skills of critical thinking and problem-solving required for competence in an empirical, science-based culture. Ready, that is, if they are solidly grounded in the embedded meanings of the preschool years and are helped to build bridges from one school experience to the next (Ashton-Warner, 1963; Delpit, 1986, 1988; Dyson, 1989; Heath, 1983, Johnson, 1987).

Beyond Early Childhood: Dialogue

To round out the picture, children beyond early childhood gradually move toward formal operational thinking in those areas of knowing in which they have solid concrete grounding, though the capacity for thinking without concrete referents remains unformed in the elementary years. Formal operations move the focus of learning to the world of ideas, in which the primary learning activity is dialogue–with other thinkers, with oneself, and with ideas in books and other media. Adolescents who have mastered the tasks of the earlier stages have the grounding they need to cope with reiteration of all the questions they previously encountered in preschool, made newly immediate by the concrete realities of puberty: Who am I? What do I want? What will I do? "There are," in Maria Piers' words, "certain phases in human development that seem characterized by a greater need for free play and daydream or fantasy. Adolescence is one, and preschool age is the other" (quoted in Paley, 1988, cover).

Adolescents' music is among the useful props for their daydreaming. For preschoolers, it's play. "Fantasy play is their ever dependable pathway to knowledge and certainty. I pretend, therefore I am. I pretend, therefore I know. I pretend, therefore I am not afraid" (Paley, 1988, p. viii).

MODES OF REPRESENTATION

Mastery of dramatic play is important in the development of representation. Representation skills culminate in becoming a writer and reader (Vygotsky, 1978). Human beings, beginning in early childhood, not only *have* experiences, they *represent* them for purposes of personal reflection, interpersonal communication, and prediction and design of future work (Forman & Fyfe, 1998). All modes of representation continue to be used throughout one's life (see Table 1.1). The primary purpose of schooling has been to ensure the acquisition of the abstract modes of literacy and numeracy. In literate societies, however, children begin the construction of their understanding of literacy long before they are formally taught.

Riding in a van with several educators through a busy village center in south Egypt, I (Gretchen) noticed a preschool-age boy sitting in a large upholstered chair behind the display case at a bread and pastries shop. The busy shopkeeper, perhaps a father, grandfather, or uncle, was serving customers. The child was drawing or writing with a big pencil on a pad in his lap. I wondered: Was this child practicing graphic and math skills that he observed adults using to keep the shop's accounts? Playing at a caregiver's side and observing while the older family member engages in the work of the day, young children are guided to participate in family work (Rogoff, 2003). Practicing tasks in the family community teaches children meaningful cultural skills at an early age.

The first mode of representation is *gesture*–body language (Vygotsky, 1978). As the infant reaches for an object, the adult interprets the reach as pointing–a gesture used to communicate–and responds as a receiver of communication. *Talk*, which follows not long after, develops in the same way, as the adult responds to babbling by interpreting it as communicative language; and the child, made much of, babbles with increasing selectivity.

Play likewise begins as exploration of the physical world. The toddler puts things in and dumps them out, picks up, stacks, and lets go. A cup may elicit the beginnings of make-believe, as the child pretends to drink from it or give a drink to a stuffed toy. As the child continues to master play, a real cup won't be necessary; if she's decided the bear is thirsty, a block or a cup that she symbolizes with a cupped hand will be sufficient to sustain the play. Children at play are re-creating familiar scripts from their social and emotional lives. Through active representation, they practice the sequences that lead to mastery.

Similarly, they first explore and then make intentional representations with two- and three-dimensional media. Markers and crayons, paint, clay, wood scraps, and blocks all serve the child in *image-making*. Scribbles are given names and move toward increasingly recognizable approximations of the thing represented. Drawing, like all other early representations, is self-corrected by the child as both his motor skills and his perceptions continue to develop.

Writing evolves as "children discover that people draw not only things, but speech" (Dyson, 1989, p. 7). Children as young as age 3 both "draw" and "write," identifying some of their scribbles as writing as they play at making signs, making lists, and writing letters (Harste, Woodward, & Burke, 1984). Both writing and reading become playscripts; becoming a reader begins not with decoding, but with the sequence, learned by watching adult readers, of picking up a book, turning it right side up, opening it, turning the pages one by one, and saying remembered words and pictures if the book is a familiar one.

Children invent writing in a process very similar to their invention of talking, if they receive a comparable response from adults (Bissex, 1980; Ferreiro & Teberosky, 1982; Harste, Woodward, & Burke, 1984). Talking begins with babbling; writing begins with scribbling, and so the provision of varied tools with which to scribble is a necessary part of the process. Early talkers move from spontaneous babble to conscious imitation of the sounds made by older talkers; similarly, early writers move from spontaneous scribbling to intentional imitation of the print in their environment. The errors made in each case are not random; they reflect the child's systems of knowledge at that point in her development. Young children are logical thinkers, though their logic may not be the adult's; they are investing their energy in constructing a mental world to make the physical world understandable.

Representation, even more than information, is what schools are about. The "basics" are still reading, writing, and 'rithmetic, and critiques of schooling typically stem from perceived deficiencies in students' mastery of these skills. These skills should indeed be learned in schools; they are not, however, well learned apart from meaningful context. "The current interest in teaching young children such things as thinking skills, learning strategies, or computer programming reflects a regression to the idea that thought and content can be treated separately. Mental processes are always content-oriented" (Elkind, 1989, p. 114). While children can be motivated to skill practice by bribes and threats (otherwise known as rewards and punishments, or positive and negative reinforcement), they learn most effectively when they perceive the learning as intrinsically interesting and useful in their lives.

Developmentally appropriate education builds on the intrinsic motivation of the child. In the preschool years, children are highly motivated to play. Work—tasks they perceive as teacher-contrived (Wing, 1995)—is of little interest, as teachers in academic preschools and kindergartens regularly discover. The myth of the short attention span of young children derives from such efforts. Young children are perfectly capable of concentrated effort over extended periods of time if what they're doing is their own idea. Children deeply engaged in a task experience "flow," which is total concentration on anything that stretches their capacity, a "fine balance between challenges and skills" (Csikszentmihalyi, 1990, p. 4). Teacher interruption of play for the purpose of teaching abstract concepts and discrete skills contradicts everything we know about the learning process of young children.

Play is not the work of the devil, as our Puritan tradition would have us believe. It is the most important activity of early childhood; in play children are at their most competent. Kindergartens, preschools, and child care centers need to be about play if they are to support growth rather than to impede it.

THE CONTENT OF PLAY

Using language, construction with materials, and their own bodies in action, children begin to represent their experiences. They improvise scripts that the observing adult can easily identify and give name to: Morning at Home, Dora the Explorer, Going to the Store, I'm Driving My Car, Feeding the Babies, Blast-off! The scripts played by the children in a preschool or kindergarten program reflect the convergence of the experience children bring with them and the materials and equipment in the school environment.

A script is a play theme based in the child's real or fantasy experiences. It is the dramatic portrayal of a sequence of events, with predictable variations. Children playing together keep it somewhat unpredictable by adding new ideas and dialogue as they negotiate the emerging script with one another. The "cooking" script may include play behaviors such as taking food from the cupboard or refrigerator, putting it in a pan, turning on the stove, stirring, turning off the stove, putting the food on a plate, putting the plate on the table as part of a table setting, and sitting down to eat. The "baby" script may include the baby's crying, picking up the baby, changing its diaper, warming a bottle, giving the bottle, burping, wrapping the baby in a blanket, taking it out in the stroller, coming home, and putting it to bed. The actor in the "driving" script gets in (on) the car, turns the key, revs the engine, turns the wheel, speeds up, jams on the brakes, and may crash! And sometimes scripts are combined as episodes in a more complicated saga such as "Driving to the Supermarket to Buy Food for Baby."

The familiarity of life's scripts is what makes the daily life of adults efficient. All the steps in the sequence have become second nature, and so we are free to think about other things as we cook or do laundry. We recognize this only when we find ourselves in an unfamiliar setting—helping set the table for lunch at someone else's house, using a different computer, taking an alternate bus route home.

Young children, new in the world as they are, play in order to find their way around in what is for them the unfamiliar country of adults, to master its daily scripts. Into this reality-based play children frequently weave fantasy themes, which give them practice with metaphors useful for representing feelings. Fantasy play enables children to experience power and mastery, to be big in imagination even though they're really little. Even adults use fantasy to compensate for and illuminate the mysteries and frustrations of daily life—which may explain the popularity of movies, videos, comics, magazines, and the array of media on the Internet.

> Watching events unfold in the dramatic play of several boys at a pre-primary school in Reggio Emilia [Italy] in the late 1990s, I named the play "Bad guys in Gotham City." I could not understand Italian, but I recognized their words "Zorro" and "Gotham City." The boys wore black capes and sparred with each other skillfully using small sticks as swords. One boy protectively carried a gunstock. The play included construction on a nearby table of a miniature Gotham City environment, made from tall tufted grasses, poppies, and packing tape. The boys stayed engaged, even after they moved outside. Later, during a roundtable discussion among visitors and teachers, I asked the teacher about the Zorro adventure play and the gunstock. What was her interpretation of the meaning of the play for the children, I wondered? Thoughtfully, she told us her role was to observe closely and be available to coach, if needed. The boys had chosen the script and directed the unfolding drama, a good thing, she said. She had permitted the child to keep his gunstock for the play, because she knew he was feeling angry. His family had left for the weekend and he was staying at his grandparents'. This play, invented, directed, and acted by the companions, was their medium for expressing mutual support and group solidarity, a source of comfort to a friend feeling lonely because his parents were away. (Reynolds, 1998, p. 7)

Pretending enables children to represent problems and practice solving them, to ask questions and learn about the world in terms they can understand. Play is self-motivated practice in meaning-making; its themes are repeated over and over until the child is satisfied that she's got this figured out. In the process she is acquiring learning strategies, knowledge, and skills. Issues of right and wrong arise as children negotiate with one another and as adults mediate. Shapes, colors, patterns, words, and numbers are embedded in the properties of dishes and blocks, puzzles and paints, trains and track, dolls and dress-ups.

MASTER PLAYERS

Effective teaching of 3- to 5-year-olds is directed toward helping them all become master players. The master player is a child who uses materials imaginatively in sustained, complex dramatic play. He is able to negotiate with others to keep the play going, working out social as well as material problems.

Two 4-year-olds were involved in this episode for 45 minutes and returned to continue it the next day:

LAURIE: Let's build an airport.
TAMARA: We need planes.
LAURIE: Let's make a tower, a big one like the one in the L.A. airport.
TAMARA: We need a lot of cars and a parking lot.
TEACHER: I like what you are making.
LAURIE: It's the airport.
TAMARA: Like the one in L.A.
TEACHER: I see that you have planes, cars, and buildings. Do you see anything else in the airport?
LAURIE: People. Can we use the little people?
TEACHER: Yes.
TAMARA: Bags. We need bags. I know! We can use the small blocks.
LAURIE: We need tickets. My mom had tickets when we went to Washington. (*She goes to cut up some papers.*)
TAMARA (*when clean-up time is announced*): Teacher, can we save this till tomorrow?

The next day they brought Barbies to school to be the mothers and sisters at the airport. More children joined them. At one point they even had the train going around the airport with people inside.

(Georgina Villarino, teacher/observer)

These are competent 4-year-olds engaged in mastering the process of inventing mutually agreed-upon representations of their experience. They are deciding what to do and how they will play it out. Through playing, they are discovering who they are, what they know, and what they want to learn next. They are practicing communication with peers: Will you play with me, and can we agree on what we're playing? They are also practicing communication with an adult as a way of asserting themselves and getting their play needs met: Can we improvise with materials, and do you value our play enough to let us continue it tomorrow? They are exercising developmentally appropriate behavior: *initiative.*

The developmental stage of initiative precedes the stage of industry (see Table 1.1, Erikson stages), in which primary-age children face the challenge of becoming competent at tasks whose rules are made by adults. The child can cope effectively when she has already experienced making up her own rules, creating her own meanings, and discovering who she is and what she knows and cares about. Self-esteem and self-concept are the outcomes of preschool play. Play enables the child to create herself as an intentional human being, unique among all human beings.

BUT WHAT DO I DO WHILE THEY'RE PLAYING?

Many adults who teach young children say they feel at a loss when children are "only playing." Some use free-choice time as a welcome opportunity to chat with other adults or to grab a cup of coffee or to prepare the next teacher-directed lesson. Others are vigilant for children's safety and quick to intervene if anything worries them, but pay little attention to the content of the play and its educational significance for children.

Teacher as Observer

This book is about paying attention to play. It focuses on the importance of play for young children ages 3 to 5 and on the skills a teacher of young children needs to support play. We emphasize that the most fundamental skill is observation, in which teachers of young children ask themselves some of these questions: What is happening for this child in this play? What is his agenda? Does he have the skills and materials he needs to accomplish his intent? To answer these questions, adults need to practice taking the child's perspective, and careful observation of children at play enables one to do just that. Observing, the teacher can try to name the play as the child might name it.

Becky, a child who typically watches or wanders rather than playing, and who hasn't left behind anything to be put away, ignores the announcement of clean-up time. After clean-up, she knows, it will be time to sit on the rug with books, so that's where she goes. She sits in front of the block shelves. Instead of picking up a book, she reaches tentatively for a block. She takes out a long block and stands it carefully on its end. It balances. She tries another, and both crash.

TEACHER (*hearing the noise*): Becky, it's not playtime now. It's clean-up time. Let's put the blocks away. (*She puts them away herself without waiting for Becky's help. Becky says something softly.*) What did you say, Becky?

BECKY: I didn't play with the toys.

TEACHER: That's okay, we all help at clean-up time. Can you help Stephanie put the dolls to bed?

She takes a passive Becky by the hand and leads her to the doll corner.

The teacher's name for this incident might be "Becky Isn't Helping." But Becky's name for it might be "What Will Happen If I Do This?" Becky's question is one regularly asked by scientists; it's a preliminary step to hypothesis-testing.

The teacher intervened to impose her rules on Becky's behavior: It's not time to play now. Everyone helps with clean-up. Sensible rules, these. And she was in a hurry, as adults often are. It was, after all, clean-up time. But Becky is a child whose lack of engaged play has been of real concern to the staff, and here she's showing a little initiative, unfortunate though her timing may be.

A teacher who was free to pause and consider Becky's motives might have thought. "She's trying to get out of clean-up. But she didn't play with anything. And now she is playing, when there's no one else in the blocks." The teacher might simply have watched to see what Becky would do next. Or she might have commented, "The blocks fell down. I wonder if you can stand them up again?" Or she might have begun thinking about ways to extend Becky's interest at a more appropriate time, perhaps by providing a protected space to build in. The adult whose priority is observing slows down to match the child's pace, exerting herself not to keep everything orderly but to ask herself the questions, "What is this play about? How can I support it?"

Imposing rules and maintaining order are part of teaching-as-managing. This is teacher behavior we all remember: "No more talking . . . pass out papers . . . do your homework now . . . time to get in line." Teaching-as-paying-attention is more difficult, more sophisticated, and more in tune with children's interests.

Primary education typically starts with questions of curriculum and method: What shall we teach the children, and how? Early childhood education has instead emphasized child study: What can we learn from the children, if we observe their naturally occurring behaviors? Piaget's observations have supported educators' discoveries that children construct knowledge for themselves through their spontaneous, intentional activity. And so, in the early years, effective teaching is based on observing. This book is full of observations–stories about real children and the adults who work with them as teachers.

Teacher as Doer

Teachers don't, however, only sit and watch play. They also make play possible. This book is organized in terms of the actions adults take to free themselves to observe children at play. Complex dramatic play typically happens when no adult is directly involved–when children are on their own in a thoughtfully planned environment, using skills and exploring interests that adults have helped them to develop.

Teachers of young children take responsibility both for the content of play and the skills–physical, emotional, cognitive, and social–that children bring to their play. Through observation, they assess each child's development, abilities, and interests, and plan what choices to make available in support of the continued development of the child's initiative in play. In this process, teachers may act in all of these roles:

Stage manager
Mediator
Player
Scribe
Assessor and communicator
Planner

Each role of the teacher is explored in depth in the chapters that follow. Chapters 2 through 4 are about the basic roles of stage manager, mediator, and player, which support children directly as they grow toward mastery of play. Behaviors that interrupt play are examined in Chapter 5. The multidimensional roles of scribe, assessor and communicator, and planner are introduced in Chapters 6 through 8.

In Chapter 9 we look at teachers' development of skills in implementing the various roles, considered in terms of the practical realities of staffing early learning programs. Finally, in Chapter 10, we return to the needs of young children in the modern world, reflecting on ways in which adults can help them build bridges of meaning among the multiple settings in which their lives unfold.

But now, the stage is set, and here comes Jenny.

CHAPTER 2

Teacher as
Stage Manager

The teacher's contribution to play always begins with the physical environment, with stage-setting. Developmentally, physical knowledge comes first. Children need the physical stuff of the world, the "It" out there that the "I" and the "Thou" find mutually interesting (Hawkins, 2002, p. 52). It's up to adults to provide enough space, enough materials, and enough time, by arranging the environment so the play can happen.

What can I do here today? Young children don't ask this question. They do it.

Jenny comes through the gate at Live Oak preschool slowly, clutching her mother's hand. On the low wall near the gate, around the edge of the sandbox, there's a beautiful collection of road-building equipment. Bright yellow dump trucks, bulldozers, and graders are neatly spaced along the wall. What 3-year-old could resist, with all that sand waiting to be dug?

Dulcie can't. She charges through the gate right behind Jenny, spots the bulldozer, and grabs it. "Mine!" she announces to the world. She plunks herself down in the sand. She bulldozes straight across the hole Marcos has been carefully digging for 5 minutes. "Hey!" he says, annoyed, and socks her. She socks him back.

The teacher approaches. "Marcos, what do you want to tell Dulcie?" she asks, squatting down between them.

But Jenny isn't interested in bulldozers or sand or arguments over territory. She stands beside her mother sucking her thumb, interested in nothing in particular. Her feelings—Do I really want to be here?—are much more compelling for her than anything in the environment.

"Want to take off your jacket and put it in your cubby?" Jenny's mother asks, hoping that Jenny will see something indoors that she wants to do. Sure enough, right next to the cubbies there's a collection of large rubber animals, sorted into traditional family groups of father, mother, and baby, parading along the shelf above the blocks. Jenny forgets about her jacket and even about her thumb.

"Look, Mommie, the baby horsie," she says happily. She takes the horse family off the shelf and settles down with them in the blocks. She's building a corral for them as her mother says goodbye.

The staff in this preschool has given a lot of attention to setting the stage for play. For the first hour of the morning, and sometimes longer, children can choose from among a variety of activities, both indoors and outdoors, when weather permits. Outdoors today there are trucks in the large sand area, paints at two easels, a variety of wheel toys, and a climbing structure with a slide. Indoors the block area has animals and small cars to use with the floor blocks. There are books and stuffed animals in a corner full of pillows, varied manipulatives on the shelves, and play dough, made of flour, salt, water, and rich brown powder paint, on the table. A home corner, partially walled off by shelves, offers child-sized kitchen and bedroom furniture, dress-up clothes both male and female, a variety of grocery items, and interesting collections of cleaning supplies and fix-it tools.

In arranging the environment, the staff has worked hard at clarifying the *figure-ground relationships.*

CLARIFYING FIGURE-GROUND RELATIONSHIPS

Remember the black-and-white drawing that keeps showing up in psychology textbooks in the chapter on perception? If you see the white as figure and the black as ground, it's a vase. If you see the black as figure and the white as ground, it's two profiles looking at each other. Your perception keeps shifting, in an interesting demonstration of the relationship between figure (what you're looking at) and ground (the background against which you see it).

Perceptual skills develop slowly, through repeated experience. For a crawling baby, depth is a new phenomenon; it takes a while to recognize, at the top of the stairs, an edge at which one should stop. On family trips in the car, if the driver suddenly says, "See that bird!" the other adults probably will, and the children probably won't; they can't yet shift their focus fast enough. Children, with much less experience, see their world less confidently, and even experienced adults can be confused by unfamiliar configurations, or by drawings designed to confuse.

To play requires the ability to choose. Making choices is easier if the figure-ground relationships are clear. "What can I do today (here in this strange place with all these people and my mommy about to leave)? Oh, I see a horsie. I like horsies. See my horsie, Mommy? . . . 'Bye, Mommy."

Jenny didn't have to look for the baby horse in a toy box or amid a jumble of other animals she hasn't yet learned to love or even to name. The preschool staff had arranged the animals carefully, each in its family group and none close enough to hostile species to risk being bitten. The baby horse was right there with its parents. The arrangement enabled Jenny to focus and made her choice easy. She didn't want lots and lots of animals; she wanted the horse family. And as she took charge of them and began building a safe fence around them, it was all right for her mommy to go. By representation in play of the relationships and feelings in their real lives, children gain a sense of mastery over them. The "macrosphere" of the larger world is beyond their control, but within the "microsphere," the small world they create in their play, they're in charge (Erikson, 1950). It's a safe place to take initiative.

Attentive teachers of young children work on clarifying figure-ground relationships throughout the day, as they support problem-solving, ask helpful questions, and pick up scraps of play dough.

For a while the play-dough table is ignored; most of the children are busy outdoors, and those indoors are involved in dramatic play. Finally a group of boys bursts in, superheroes needing the bathroom and their water bottles. One of them spots the new brown play dough.

"Look, doo-doo!" he exults. The others are quick to follow his lead: "Ca-ca." "Poo-poo." "Ca-ca poo-poo," yells the most imaginative. They crowd around the table. "Is that really poo-poo?" Matthew asks the teacher doubtfully.

"What do you think?" she asks. "How could you find out?"

"Poo-poo stinks! Stinky, stinky poo-poo," chants Brad. But Matthew ignores Brad; he's really curious. "I don't think you'd put poo-poo on the table," he decides. "I think it's play dough." He sits down and touches it tentatively.

"Yuck! Stinky poo-poo," yells Brad, trying to keep his fascinating theme going. But he's lost it. The teacher ignores his bathroom talk, and the other children's curiosity and pleasure in play dough take over. Two more boys join Matthew at the table. Brad wanders off, looking for some new action.

Play dough and table knives keep Matthew, Zach, and Warren absorbed for 10 minutes. The conversation turns quickly to doughnuts and grilling meat patties. The teacher sits with the boys for a few minutes, then moves on to the other areas.

When she returns, the boys have left; Brad swooped by and enticed them into a superhero chase. They have left the table strewn with the remains of their work. A student observer is sitting nearby, and the teacher sits down at the table to talk with her. As they talk, the teacher fiddles with the play dough, shaping dough into pancakes, making a pile of them. Then she starts rolling up the stray bits of play dough, snowball fashion. Pretty soon there's a whole row of dough balls on the table.

Camilla arrives. "How did you make those?" The teacher demonstrates. Camilla picks up a knife and starts slicing one of the balls into pancakes. Rosie arrives and wants to make pancakes, too, but there's only one knife to be found.

"Could you use the tortilla press to make pancakes?" the teacher asks, getting it off the shelf. "No pancakes. *Tortillas, sí*" says Rosie happily. Lots of tortillas.

The teacher is rolling another ball as Brad arrives, out of breath and full of energy. He seems to have forgotten about poo-poo. "What are you doing?" he asks. "I'm making a ball," she replies. He gives her a challenging look, then raises his fist and smashes the ball. She admires his superhero strength, and tells him so: "You made a pancake."

So he did. He reaches for another ball and flattens it, too. He wants another, and she shows him how to make one. Now they're both rolling dough around.

Marcos arrives. He takes all the remaining balls to make a snow person. His pile gets so high that he has to squish them onto each other so they won't fall down. Then he puts a pancake hat on top and pulls it down, droopy-mushroom fashion, inviting the teacher to admire it. She does.

This teacher habitually brings order to the environment as she moves through it. Before she gets to the play dough, she has picked up two dolls from the floor and put them back to bed, hung up a fire hat, and spent a few minutes shelving scattered blocks. But a student teacher asks her about picking up blocks: "That's the children's job."

"Yes, it is," the teacher agrees. "They need to help with clean-up. But right now it's still playtime, and I want them to be able to see clearly what's here to play with."

"But when you straighten things, the kids just mess them up," objects the student.

"I know. That's why I do it," grins the teacher, as she picks bits of old, dry dough out of a garlic press.

What this teacher does is to keep reestablishing clear figure-ground relationships, spontaneously creating order out of disorder to make the possibilities clear to children. If they "mess up" (use and change) what she has provided, she knows she's succeeded in supporting their play. Their order is always different from hers. And the classroom is theirs, not hers; she sets it up so they can re-create it.

In a meeting with placement students at day's end, she wants to explain her thinking after Beth has wondered, "Why do we have to put everything out so neatly when the kids don't have to keep it that way?"

"What I want to do is create a logically ordered presentation of materials that will make sense to the children," the teacher says slowly, choosing her words as she thinks about the question. "If they know where to find things, they can focus their energies on using materials in play."

"But they're messing up the order," protests Noemi. "This morning I must have spent fifteen minutes sorting out all the dress-up clothes and putting them where they belong, and you know where they ended up? In a great big jumbled pile in the wagon, in the corner of the yard under the trees. The whole family picked up and moved to Mexico–that was what they were playing–and practically everything from the house corner went along with them. All my work wasted!"

"Hey, but the play was great," says John, who had helped the movers get the wagon out the door and off the porch. "I was taking notes on what they said. The grandparents came to meet them when they got to Mexico, and they went straight to a wedding. Those dress-ups did get used, Noemi. Everyone put on all the clothes they could find."

"They messed up your order, Noemi, so they could transform it into their own," says the teacher. "If this were your house, you might choose not to let them do that (though that can be a constant struggle between parents and children at home). But this isn't a home; it's a preschool for children. It's their place, not ours. Our job is to make it work for them.

"When it ends up looking messy, that's usually a sign that we've succeeded–that the children are using the materials abundantly to support their own 'wonderful ideas' [Duckworth, 2007]. The stuff that's around is like that in a chef's kitchen or an artist's studio, left in the wake of the creation of a masterpiece."

"Like my desk when I finished that last paper!" says John.

"That makes sense," says Beth. "But it turns us into housekeepers, doesn't it? I don't know that I like being a housekeeper. Besides, they've got to learn about chores before kindergarten."

"I'm a terrible housekeeper at home," says the teacher, "but I have to be a diligent one at preschool or the play deteriorates. It's the adults, not the children, who are responsible for the larger picture, the overall order of the play environment. As the children create new order, their own order–a block tower, a painting, play-dough tortillas, a doll tucked carefully into bed–the surroundings get cluttered with leftover blocks, a painting still on the easel, scraps of dough, and doll blankets on the floor. So, as you've noticed, while children are playing, I do a lot of low-key picking up and putting away.

"You know all the discussions we've had about the differences between open and closed materials? Open materials allow many approaches [Lewin-Benham, 2010], and they can be combined and recombined in any number of ways, stimulating children's imaginations. To make a puzzle, which is closed, the child has to be able to put the pieces together in their right order. But completion of an open task occurs whenever the child is satisfied with the order she has invented.

"At clean-up time, which happens after play time is over, we reestablish our order. The purpose of our order is to help children get started and keep focused in play, both of which depend on the balance between too much complexity and not enough. Were you watching Jenny this morning? For her, the balance offered by the animals in family groups was just right; thank you, John, for setting those up so nicely. She could see the possibilities and get started, which she couldn't have done if they'd all been jumbled in a toy box. And if they'd been pieces in a puzzle, I don't think that would have worked, either. Jenny was already anxious about her mom's leaving; she didn't need the anxiety she would feel if she were trying to do a closed task right. Open materials in a suggested order—the adults' order that need not be maintained—leave the most room for children to create their own ideas in play."

PROVIDING ENOUGH PROPS

We're fond of this next story about children's play outdoors when Second Street School teachers introduced loose parts, and we decided to retain it in this second edition, although we know that it's dated. Safety standards now define acceptable numbers of young children using an area and require fencing; and asphalt surfaces are obsolete, replaced by eco-friendly surfaces, natural materials, and beautiful spaces with unlimited potential for children's learning (Keeler, 2008).

Second Street School has two preschool classes that share a large asphalt play yard with a kindergarten class. Early in the fall, when an observer begins visiting regularly, it's evident that the teachers of all three classes have given thought to the organization of their classrooms, but not yet to the shared outdoor space.

September

There are thirty 3- and 4-year-olds outdoors. The stationary equipment includes four swings and several climbers and slides. There is a large expanse of sand under the permanent structure, and a lone frisbee. Children are climbing, sliding, swinging, waiting for turns on the swings, running, and throwing sand. Four children are playing with the frisbee. Three boys are wrestling in the sand. There is a bike path painted on the asphalt; several children are running around it. A boy discovers that if he uses his heels, the slide makes a fine loud drum, but an adult tells him to stop.

A running child falls and skins her knee. She cries loudly. "Why is she crying?" one adult asks another. "She was running," is the accusing answer.

The observer is uncomfortable seeing all these children without enough to do to keep them either happy or safe. From her viewpoint, the only imaginative play in the yard, which the observer names Run Away and Hide!, has been organized by two small boys who are hiding in the bushes, then running around the corner and along the covered walkway adjacent to the yard. They are entirely out of sight of any adult. They disappear and reappear; it is some time before they are caught at this unacceptable game.

By the time children have been outside for 25 minutes, some are asking to go in for lunch. But it isn't lunchtime. "I can break down the door," the observer hears one boy say to his suitably impressed friends. Several children waiting on the porch begin a running game until a teacher arrives to organize them into a line and take them in.

Early October

All three classes are outside, for a total of at least 45 children. Teachers have brought out bikes and a hoop. Many children are waiting for turns. Complaints of "Teacher!" are frequently heard. It's been windy, and the porch and the dirt under the trees are covered with leaves.

The observer, back for another visit, foresees another frustrating morning for everyone. Because she's had some chance to get acquainted with the preschool teachers in weekly seminars they've been having together, she decides to risk stepping out of strict observer behavior. "Would it be all right," she asks one of the teachers, "if I brought out a few crates and the zoo animals from the block area in the room?" The teacher, surprised but curious, thinks about the idea and then agrees.

The observer puts the crates on the porch, stands up several animals in a crate, and puts the remaining animals with the leaves under the trees. "What are those for?" asks a child, immediately curious. "I thought they might like to come outside in the leaves," says the visitor. "Can we play with them?" the child asks. And play they do—zoo, animal growl, bury animals in the leaves, take them for a bike ride, wash them in the drinking fountain. Animal-washing is particularly absorbing for several children over a long period of time.

Enterprising children from the other preschool class go into their room and bring out their animals—and a few cars for good measure. Oh, oh, the two rooms' animals are going to get mixed up, thinks the observer. How nice, a cooperative classification activity in the making, is her second thought. Our animals, your animals. She suggests the idea to the other teacher. As she leaves, she wonders what will be happening on her next visit—or whether she'll even be welcome.

Late October

The observer, apparently welcome, returns to spend some time in the other preschool room. At the end of circle time the teacher asks the children, "What would you like to bring outside?" "Animals," says one boy, and they do.

Outdoors, the sand table is filled with birdseed, not sand, and lots of tools. There is also a crate full of tools that children can take to use in the sand around the base of the climbers. There are trikes and wagons, tin-can stilts, a ball, and leaves. The preschool teacher across the way has spread a gym mat on the porch against the classroom wall, added two lacy pillows, a quilt, and some dolls to make a large bed, and now is sitting comfortably on it in the sun. One girl is snuggled next to her, talking; two others are tucking dolls into bed.

Again the drinking fountain gets used for washing animals. Some children bring containers from the sand to fill with water; wet sand is much more useful than dry sand. Later in the morning brooms, dust pans, and a trash can are brought out by a teacher and used enthusiastically by children. There are lots of leaves to be swept.

This morning, with many things to do and with adult attentiveness to play, outdoor play goes on for an hour and no one asks if it's time to go in. Everyone loses track of the time, in fact, until a teacher notices in surprise that it's lunchtime.

The staff had set up an environment outdoors that permitted all kinds of play and language to flourish. The teacher permitted children to help create the environment—to bring out things they thought they would need and to go back in for more. Water play, spilling, combining and recombining materials, noise, moving one's body in many different ways, even washing sandy animals in the drinking fountain (which may have been against school rules but nobody wanted to check) were permitted. Nobody got hurt, and "Teacher!" didn't get yelled so often. By adding props, teachers had transformed an environment that had not been working for children or adults into an environment that was interesting and pleasant for everyone.

Play needs plenty of props (although children who have mastered pretend play have less need for them than beginning players do [Smilansky & Shefatya, 1990, pp. 55, 72]). Without enough to do, children hurt themselves and each other, practice creative rule-breaking, and fuss or become lethargic. Adults find themselves policing rather than supporting play. With plenty of "loose parts" (Nicholson, 1974) that can be combined and recombined and that support the creation of complex playscripts, play goes on and on. Note that loose parts are lightweight objects of different sizes, shapes, and textures that children can manipulate and move from place to place. Organic materials, such as sand and water, and moveable boards and ramps encourage flexibility, novelty, and challenge.

In this preschool even the observer, who knew about the theory of loose parts, was astonished at how much difference additional materials made. Teachers had thought it would be too much work to take things outside, but the children were eager to help and were ready with requests for new items they thought might be interesting to take outside.

Once the children had enough to do, supervising their play became both easy and fun. Staff were no longer policing; instead, they had become property managers on a lively stage, and the play was a stellar production.

PROVIDING ENOUGH TIME

Stage managers are concerned with time as well as space and props. The more scene changes there are, the more entrances and exits, the harder the manager's task. Like plays in the theater, programs for young children vary greatly in structure and pace. In a 3-hour, half-day program or a 10- to 12-hour child care day, the tempo may be relaxed or hurried, individualized or regimented. In some programs, the staff spends much time managing scene changes.

At Little Friends, a church-based child care program not far from Second Street School, three preschool classrooms share, on a rotating schedule, several common spaces: a small play yard, downstairs and outside; a large gym, upstairs (used in the evenings as a community recreation center); and a bathroom down the hall, which is also used by adults at work in the church offices and meeting rooms. Children are expected to move among these spaces in lines, ensuring reasonably orderly behavior in the halls. The day is tightly scheduled to make the space usable.

In keeping with the program's philosophy, group times are more valued than playtimes. The unhurried times of the day take place during meals and sharing circles, where adults sit with children and encourage conversation. Playtimes typically last for only half an hour, and clean-up follows each one. Children are free to play during less than a third of the day.

At Live Oak child care center, scheduling is quite different. There are four long blocks of time during the day when children are free to begin and end their own activities. The physical space facilitates this scheduling; bathrooms are in the classrooms, and there is direct access to the outdoors, making possible independent toileting and free indoor-outdoor movement. In addition, the scheduling reflects a conscious effort by staff to provide a relaxed pace and to interrupt children no more than necessary. For more than half the day, children are free to play.

Both morning and afternoon snacks are a choice, made available for half an hour or more until all interested children have eaten. As at Little Friends, group times serve to smooth transitions from one space to another, but once children are in a space they may choose freely for 1 to 2 hours. The long midday time when children don't choose—clean-up, lunch, and rest—has been planned so that morning and afternoon staff overlap to provide individualized attention to children and all the flexibility possible.

Live Oak, which has adopted the ideal of "day care as a good home" (Prescott, 1978), values the child's lived time more highly than the conveniences of institutional time. Little Friends, in contrast, could have been described by Suransky (1982) in *The Erosion of Childhood.*

The concept of allowing a child to complete an activity he was engaged in was subordinate to the compelling nature of the *schedule,* which the teachers planned in advance of the children's experiences. The strict demarcation of the morning, by its very organization, denied the children the possibility of a continuous, uninterrupted activity brought to its natural closure. Instead, the structure was believed efficient by the staff (which indeed it was) and was intended to give the children a sense of security and consistency. While the children did appear to derive security from the temporal rigidity, they clearly became dependent on the structure and felt uncomfortable with any deviation. (p. 61)

Time, it is clear, can be managed in many ways. Some ways are responsive to young children's erratic pace and to the wide variation in pace among individuals, supporting autonomy and enabling children to exert initiative in largely uninterrupted play. Other ways are clock-controlled and group-focused, attempting to move all the children together. In such programs children get practice for the constraints they may later find in public school, but restricted opportunity to practice the initiative that is the developmental challenge for competent 3- to 5-year-olds.

Conformity to schedules and clock time is inappropriate preschool curriculum. In one experiment with "untiming the curriculum," the teachers agreed to remove the clock and did not wear watches, paying attention instead to children's rhythms and pacing. Focused play was not interrupted; the curriculum expanded and learning deepened. One boy had time to figure out the construction of a bridge with blocks. For a month several children were engaged with a babies curriculum (Wien & Kirby-Smith, 1998). Children's own rhythms, the adults discovered, are important to honor in planning the day.

Synchrony—precisely coordinated timing—is a basic characteristic of industrial society (Toffler, 1980). It is no historic accident that the clock has dominated the schoolroom wall and that every day in most kindergartens begins with "calendar." But as society moves from the rigidity of the assembly line to the flexibility made possible by information technology, our children may be better served by schooling that fosters their exploration and initiative, instead of schooling that fosters unquestioning obedience to clocks and calendars.

Obedience is a virtue in a stable society where the unexpected doesn't often happen. But in a rapidly changing society, children have greater need for confidence in the face of new problems to be solved. Children regularly encounter problems in their dealings both with the physical world and with other human beings, big and little. Teachers can help them to become increasingly independent problem-solvers.

An animal that depends on the accumulated knowledge of past generations has to have some time to acquire that knowledge. An animal that depends on imagination has to have time to exercise it. Childhood is that time . . . . When we're children we're devoted to learning about our world and imagining all the other ways that world could be. When we become adults we put all that we've learned and imagined to use. (Gopnik, 2009, p. 11)

CHAPTER 3

Teacher
as Mediator

"Now, what do you do if you have any trouble with a friend?" asked the smiling teacher reviewing the kindergarten rules with the class.

"Tell the teacher," volunteered a boy.

"That's right," agreed the teacher. "Come straight to Mrs. Jordan, and she'll help you. Don't try to do it without my help. Teachers are here to help children be friends and work together nicely."

Predictably, "Teacher!" was often heard in this classroom, and the teacher could be counted on to solve children's problems for them. This approach teaches trust in helpful adults and dependence on them for resolving problems. In contrast, teachers of young children whose goal is the development of independent problem-solving skills sometimes adopt a laissez-faire approach: "Don't come to me. You figure it out." More effective, in modeling and explaining problem-solving skills that children can later practice on their own, is the role of teacher-as-*mediator*.

TEACHING CONFLICT-RESOLUTION SKILLS

Young children at play frequently run afoul of each other in ways they can't handle on their own. Their agendas don't match, and they get in each other's way; sometimes the results are explosive. To protect them and, in the process, teach them conflict-resolution skills they can use independently with each other, adult mediation is essential.

In Chapter 2, at Live Oak preschool we saw Dulcie encountering a bulldozer. "Mine!" she announced. But she wasn't the only worker in the sandbox. Bulldozing, she turned Marcos's "figure"—his carefully dug hole—into her "ground," just part of the landscape to be flattened. Preschoolers do this a lot. Intent on their own play, they fail to notice that they've invaded someone else's territory. Marcos noticed; he socked Dulcie. Dulcie, surprised and indignant, socked him back.

John, a student teacher, saw them, and a series of possible reactions flashed through his mind. "Don't hit girls," his big brother would have said, but that's not what you say in preschool. When John himself attended day care as a child, time-out would have been the next step, but for which child, he wondered—Marcos, Dulcie, or both? *Here, no one uses time-out, so what am I supposed to say? "We don't hit. Use your words." . . . and then what will they do?*

While John was thinking, the teacher, who had also seen the incident, moved in.

"Marcos, what do you want to tell Dulcie?" she asks, squatting down between them. Marcos is crying; Dulcie socked him hard. Dulcie is annoyed; the teacher is in her bulldozer's way, a much more formidable obstacle than Marcos.

"I don't *like* her. She's a dumb-dumb," sobs Marcos.

"You're mad at Dulcie. Can you tell her what she did to make you mad?"

"Hit me," says Marcos, sadly.

"You hit me first," says Dulcie, reasonably.

"Marcos, did you hit Dulcie?" the teacher asks. He nods.

"Why?"

"My hole!" he wails, the memory of the violation of his play suddenly much more painful than the sore spot on his shoulder. "She messed my hole!" He tries to hit Dulcie again.

"What hole?" asks Dulcie, genuinely puzzled. "I didn't mess no hole."

"Can you show Dulcie your hole, Marcos?" the teacher asks. He certainly can. "Here!" he shouts. "It was right here, and I digged it and digged it . . . ."

"Dulcie, Marcos is really sad about his hole," explains the teacher. "Do you think maybe you could help him fix it?" Dulcie nods vigorously, grabbing her bulldozer.

"No!" says Marcos. "No 'dozer!"

"Do you want to fix the hole yourself, Marcos?" the teacher asks. He nods yes. "Then could you show Dulcie where to drive her bulldozer so she won't mess up your hole again?"

Marcos sketches a wide detour with his outstretched arm. Dulcie, following it, bulldozes off. Marcos wields his shovel, and his very important hole begins to take shape once more.

By focusing on the content of the play rather than on the violation of rules (We don't hit), the teacher has shown respect for both children's intent. She has used words to help them solve their very real problem and continue their play. The play is the important thing that's happening; problem-solving strategies should give priority to its continuation. In contrast, time-out—stop playing and sit by yourself and think about what you've done—destroys the play and does not give young children useful strategies for solving either this problem or the next one that comes along.

In her role as mediator, the teacher asked genuine questions that enabled the children to use their words in effective communication to her and to each other. Among animals, children, and nations, territorial problems often lead to conflict. Here, Dulcie hadn't even noticed Marcos's territorial problem. They're only 3-year-olds, and he hasn't learned how to tell her. His teacher helped. By asking, "What do you want to tell Dulcie?," she suggested words as an alternative to both crying and hitting. Such suggestions, backed up by physical protection, build for the child a repertoire of his own strategies to draw on in times of need.

In territorial disputes, skilled teachers use clearly ordered words, as well as clearly ordered materials, to help children see figure-ground relationships: Dulcie, this is Marcos's hole. He really wants his hole right where he dug it. Can your road go way around his hole? He'll show you where.

Dulcie finds that reasonable, and way 'round she goes. Her bulldozer likes going way 'round. She didn't mean to mess Marcos's hole. She just didn't know it was there.

COMPLICATING PLAY TO KEEP IT SAFE

Having mediated this dispute, the teacher was free to move on to another activity. Scanning the yard to see where everyone was, she recognized she might be needed indoors. There she found the play-dough table deserted, but when she sat down to greet an observer, children joined her. While rolling balls of dough, she suddenly wondered, "Why couldn't Rosie find a knife to slice her play dough? True, the tortilla press proved to be an inspiration, but where are those knives? And what are Matthew, Zach, and Warren up to, since they used those knives last? (See Chapter 2.) Are the heroes armed?"

The teacher goes to see. She finds the boys and knives by the art supplies, where the boys have gone for string. Warren has wrapped string 'round and 'round his pants leg to hold the plastic knife snugly against it, ready to hand in case of danger. Zach is struggling to cut Warren's string from the ball so he, in turn, can have a sheath like Warren's.

"What are you making?" the teacher asks.

"Brad, he's Shredder," explains Matthew eagerly. "He's the bad guy. The very bad guy. We scared him with our knives and he ran away. [*No wonder Brad was smashing play dough,* thinks the teacher.] We scared him. We scared him good. But he might come back. We're getting our knives ready for him."

"I'll bet he was really scared," says the teacher, "if you threatened him with those real knives. I'd be scared, too. I don't think he knew you were pretending. What did he do that was bad?"

"He dumped our doughnuts!" says Matthew indignantly. "We made 'em and we made 'em, and we were gonna eat 'em, and he yelled poo-poo and dumped 'em off the table and ran. So we took those knives and we scared him good! We scared him all over. We let him get away, though."

"Did anyone see you chasing Brad with knives?" asks the teacher, startled by this revelation. Where were the adults supervising the room?

"Oh, we hid the knives," Matthew explains reassuringly. "Teachers don't like knives. We just showed them at Brad, and boy, was he scared!"

"Real scared!" confirms Zach.

"That's why we're stringing them on," says Warren. "They hide better that way."

Concealed weapons, thinks the teacher. *Now that's all we need.* "Why did Brad dump your doughnuts?" she asks.

"Shredder's bad!" they chorus. "Brad, he's Shredder and he's bad!"

"Does Shredder ever get hungry?" wonders the teacher. "Do you suppose Brad was hungry and wanted a doughnut, and you had all the doughnuts, and he was trying to get one?"

"No, Shredder's just bad," Matthew insists.

"I'm hungry," says Zach. "We need some more doughnuts. Let's go, Turtles!"

"Can Brad have some doughnuts, too?" the teacher asks.

"He can be Leonardo," Matthew decides. "He's not Shredder anymore. Hey, Brad, you're Leonardo! Want a doughnut? We're making doughnuts."

The teacher offers, "Let's look through the basket of tools together. Brad, will you help? I bet we can find a garlic press and a pizza cutter for making fancy doughnuts. And maybe a cutter for doughnut holes."

Though the Ninja Turtles may have become less popular since this story was first told, 4- and 5-year-old superhero and antihero play goes on and on. Our discussion about "good and bad guy" and war play reflects the ideas of Paley (1984, 1986a, 1990), Levin (2008, 2009), and the NAEYC position statement *Media Violence in Children's Lives* (1994).

In the role of mediator, had the teacher seen Brad actually threatened with knives, even blunt plastic knives, she would have intervened at once to keep everyone safe. Instead she missed that part of the action and was inadvertently available at the play-dough table when she realized that Matthew, Warren, and Zach had taken off with the play-dough knives and were intending to use them aggressively.

Toy weapons are unavailable as play props in this program, and the children were scheming to use the knives as weapons, concealing them in sheaths, probably an idea they imitated from television-watching or a movie. Responsible first for children's physical and emotional safety (Levin, 2008), the teacher intercepted them as they were cutting string for sheaths. She was able to resist the temptation to impose adults' rules—no chasing, no threatening, the knives stay at the table, TIME-OUT! Rather than assuming what was going on, she showed them she respected their ideas by asking authentic questions about the script. Understanding it enabled her to match her guidance to its rules. Her suggestion that Shredder might have been hungry was first rejected by Matthew—"No, Shredder's just bad"—but it made a connection with Zach, who was ready for more doughnut-baking. Outfoxed by a good idea, Matthew capitulated gracefully and invited Brad back into the play he had rejected earlier. And the knives went back to the play-dough table, where they belonged. The teacher stayed alert so they didn't get taken off again. Through her forbearance, the play continued—it did not get sabotaged by the aggressive subplot. As mediator, she was able to expand the children's understanding through genuine questioning (Paley, 1986b) rather than shame them through moralizing.

Teacher-as-mediator is not simply managing behavior; she is teaching social skills and suggesting ideas to enrich play. Her goals include the development of both empathy and divergent thinking. Adults as mediators can scaffold children's positive behaviors from inside a dramatic playscript. Time-out is externally imposed behavior management. It removes the child from the play and does not give practice in expressing feelings, identifying problems, and considering peaceful solutions (Levin, 2008). Children this young can begin to learn social consciousness, and their real problems are a meaningful context.

If her goal were to teach independent problem-solving, a teacher-as-mediator might invite all four boys to come together to discuss the conflict, to listen to each other's feelings, and to suggest ideas for coming up with a mutually agreeable resolution (Eaton, 1997). Intentional teaching includes guiding play when children themselves do not realize that their actions may be unsafe or hurtful. Here is an imagined scenario where the teacher coaches the boys in independent problem-solving.

The teacher finds Zach, Warren, and Matthew at the art supplies, engaged in designing sheaths for knives. She explains that she noticed the knives missing from the play-dough table, and asks about their idea. Matthew says that Brad is the bad guy, he's Shredder, because he interfered with their doughnut-making when he dumped them on the floor. The teacher asks Brad to join this conversation so he can be part of the solution. "Brad, will you tell us what happened?"

Warren, Matthew, Zach, and the teacher are listening to Brad. "I wanted to play Ninjas make pizza, cause that's what they really do, on television! But Matthew and Zach wanted lots of doughnuts, and so I dumped 'em, I shredded 'em. They grabbed those knives like numchops and chased me! I was scared, real scared."

The teacher says, "Zach, Matthew, Warren, and Brad, can you together decide how to play together peacefully?"

Matthew says, "Maybe just play Ninjas outside where we can run and chase and play scary stuff?"

"Yeah!" says Warren.

Brad replies, "Then it's scary outdoors, too."

Zach offers to have Brad join them. "Hey, we are hungry for lots of doughnuts. Four boys can be bakers. Teacher, will you get us one more knife? Then we'll have four. I know how to make doughnut holes. I'll show you!"

Warren says, "Hey, I need the garlic press to make coconut for the top."

Brad returns happily with them to the play-dough table.

Why all the good guys and bad guys? The popular media entrenched in most families' lives surround children, at home and in public places, with screens depicting violence. Toy replicas of screen characters marketed everywhere are typically single-purpose, so children don't play with them creatively; they simply imitate screen scenarios. (Levin, 2009; NAEYC, 1994). They are learning someone else's lessons—i.e., the scriptwriter's—about who are the good and bad guys and what good and bad guys do. "They are not exploring their own ideas, working out their own solutions to problems, being creative and imaginative in their own unique ways, but rather are being programmed by someone else" (Levin, 2009, p. 50).

PROBLEM-SOLVING TO SUSTAIN PLAY

The teacher mediates between children and also between a child and the sometimes recalcitrant physical world. String and dull scissors may simply be too much for a preschooler and require direct assistance. But a child tugging at a wagon whose wheel is wedged behind a board can be helped to notice the source of the problem and thus to solve it for herself. David Hawkins (2002) has described this kind of help as "completing the circuit" for children. He proposes an electronic analogy:

> Think of circuits that have to be completed. Things go out along one bundle of channels, something happens, and signals come back along another bundle of channels; and there's some sort of feedback involved. Children are not always able to sort all of this feedback for themselves. The adult's function, in all the child's learning, is to provide a kind of external loop, to provide a selective feedback from the child's own choice and action. The child's involvement gets some response from an adult and this in turn is

made available to the child. The child is learning about himself through his joint effects on the non-human and the human world around him.

The function of the teacher, then, is to respond diagnostically and helpfully to a child's behavior, to make what he considers to be an appropriate response, a response which the child needs to complete the process he's engaged in at a given moment. (p. 56)

There are frequent periods, Hawkins makes clear, when children don't need the external loop. But

When they do need it and there's no one around to contribute the adult resonance, then they're not always able to carry on the process of investigation, of inquiry and exploration, of learning, because they need help over a hump that they can't surmount through their own resources. If help isn't available, the inquiry will taper off, and that particular episode, at least, will have failed to accomplish what it otherwise might have. (p. 57)

What kinds of "humps" do children encounter as they play? How can adults help?

At Second Street child care center the outdoor environment for the 3-year-olds is well provisioned with a climber, bikes, a sand area with tools, a playhouse, and a number of milk crates. The children have dispersed to the various activities. A girl and two boys have started a chase game. Several children have attached themselves to their teacher. They hold her hands as she walks around the yard, a reassuring presence, talking with children in a friendly way, helping to sort out traffic jams on the bike path. For a short while she pulls a wagon with two children in it. "Victor, are you all right?" she calls, moving in his direction as he yells from across the yard. Her message is consistent: I'm paying attention; you can tell me how you're feeling.

Now she is helping Marina, Ebony, and Annie organize crates into a street vending space, at which they sell things—tickets to the beach and to Disneyland, and ice cream, as the play develops—to the passersby. As the teacher moves on, the assistant teacher arrives. They sell him a ticket and give him change. He helps them rebuild the crates, two of which have fallen.

Marina: Knock-knock.

Assistant Teacher (*moving another crate*): Oh, knock-knock on the door? Now you've got doors. (*Marina gives him directions, then tells him something else.*) Can I have change? Got something else to drink? You can stop Ruben when he comes by and give him a ticket. Ruben, you can stop there and get your ticket.

THE GIRLS (*to Ruben, on his bike*): Ruben. (*He comes for a ticket, and they turn
   to Ricky.*) Ricky, want a ticket? (*He speeds by without stopping.*)
ASSISTANT TEACHER: Okay, is the door back there? How are you?
MARINA: Fine.

Traffic on the path increases. A heavy load goes by—a boy on a bike with
a trailer, with a girl in the trailer pulling two more boys in a wagon! Hearing a
squabble at a concession booth, the assistant teacher responds, "Don't tease her.
You sell your tickets, and she can sell hers." A boy joins the ticket sellers. There's
an argument over territory. The assistant teacher tells one of the girls, "Tell 'em
you had it first."

Less skilled players, a category that includes many 3-year-olds, are
helped to sustain the focus of their play by adult ideas, physical assistance–
the crates are big and bulky–and intervention in disputes. This teacher assistant, who used to moralize a lot (see Chapter 5), is learning to enter into
play and to keep it foremost as he helps with problem-solving. By modeling
appropriate behavior, he helps children keep the play going. When some of
his interventions are less skilled, the teacher models for the children and for
him, too.

The block area is supplied with a dozen large pieces of heavy cardboard—
dismantled packing boxes—a wonderful resource for creating little houses of one's
own. In a small space with 3-year-olds, some of whom hit instead of using words,
territory is a frequent issue. There are many opportunities for problem-solving.

ASSISTANT TEACHER (*responding to a dispute*): Victor, what are you doing to Andy?
   Don't do that. (*Andy, unsatisfied, goes over to the teacher.*)
TEACHER (*hugging Andy*): Andy doesn't like that, Victor. He's very upset. It hurts
   him when you do that. (*To Andy.*) Do you want a drink of water?
RUBEN (*in dress-ups, succeeding after a struggle to get a dress on*): Teacher,
   lookit.
TEACHER: Oh boy, are you dressed to the nines! Look at that red dress. (*Hearing
   a wail from the cardboard houses.*) Tell Jerry you need your blanket back.
   Annie needs her blanket back, Jerry. (*To Andy, who has put on a flowered
   skirt.*) You got a new outfit.

The teacher soothes Annie, who has followed her. She helps Annie fix a new
space for herself and gets her a soft rabbit and a blanket. When Marina comes over
to play, the teacher demonstrates for her: "Here's the door. Knock. Knock-knock.
Can I come in?"

On this morning both adults were able to be playful. They were giving information to the children about materials and ideas for their play and

about getting along with each other, but they were doing so as co-players rather than in a teacher-like fashion. When adults intervene within the script, children are helped to sustain it.

These were young 3-year-olds at the beginning of the day care year. They were exploring the physical environment, first and foremost, with some successful forays into sustained dramatic play. Here they needed, and got, lots of help from the adults, who were working hard. Continual involvement is necessary at the beginning of the year, when it's up to adults to help children learn how to play with the materials and with each other—to socialize them into the culture of child care. And to reassure them that this is a safe place to be, with caring adults.

CHAPTER 4

Teacher
as Player

When should an adult participate in children's play? The adults in the 3-year-old class described in Chapter 3 moved in and out of play to model and mediate. They acted as builder's helper, customer of the street vendors, admirer of new fashion, and visitor knocking at the door. In all these roles, they helped to sustain the play while responding to children's ideas.

"CALL MIKEY"

At Live Oak child care center, another teacher imaginatively role-played solutions to a pretend homemaker's real problem.

As the teacher approaches the play kitchen, Paula tells him the oven door won't close.

TEACHER: Call someone to come and fix it.
PAULA (*phone in hand*): What's the number?
TEACHER (*one number at a time as Paula dials*): 282-4761.
PAULA (*into phone*): Can you come and fix our stove? He says yes.
TEACHER: How much does he charge?
PAULA: What do you charge? (*calling to the teacher*) $1,500.
TEACHER: $1,500! Oh no, tell him no. Call Mikey.
PAULA: What number?
TEACHER: 792-3594.
PAULA (*into phone*): Mikey, can you come fix our stove? (*Calling to teacher.*) He says yes!
TEACHER: Is he coming? What does he charge?
PAULA: $3.00.
TEACHER: That's better. (*Alan comes into the kitchen.*) Are you Mikey?
ALAN: Yes!

Deciding whether or not to participate in children's play requires thought about children's need for challenge, their skills in sustaining play, and one's own preferred teaching style. Some skilled teachers feel that an adult's place is outside the play. Some look for opportunities to add materials or ideas. Some join in frequently; they like to play, and they feel that their participation builds relationships with children and enriches the content of the play.

"DON'T LET THE BABIES DIE"

The preschool in the following episode has a prop box of medical supplies in frequent use. Several weeks earlier the teacher was an active participant in hospital play, helping Sarah use CPR to resuscitate her doll, Bubbles. Today the dolls are sick again.

Sarah begins by explaining, "Bubbles is sick, and her brother, Pea-pod. This is the only girl who is not sick. Her name is Heather." Lia and Liana go to the house area and bring many blankets, while Sarah builds with hollow blocks. She gets the plastic ironing board, which had previously served as an operating table for Bubbles.

LIA: We got a pillow for her.

SARAH: I need to put her in my safe house.

LIANA: Lots of people work on a baby that has this. They check her heart. Use the stick.

SARAH: She has CPR. Her heart is beating too fast. She might throw up.

JOSEPH (*very seriously*): I don't think your baby is going to be all right. She's going to have to go to heaven.

SARAH (*smiling*): I know!

JOSEPH: I saw a huge cut on her.

SARAH: I think both our babies are going to die.

TEACHER: That would be so sad.

TRAVIS: Don't let the babies die.

LIANA: We shouldn't let Sarah's die. That would make her so sad.

TEACHER: What about the other one?

LIANA: We should try not to let that one die either. I'm working on some stuff. (*She wraps a syringe and some medical supplies in a piece of paper.*)

SARAH: She has a bigger cut than we thought.

LIANA: I'm wrapping a message up from on the surgery.

TEACHER: When is surgery?

SARAH: Surgery is after snack.

TEACHER: Will she be okay?
SARAH: Yes!

(Linda Torgerson, teacher observer)

In her earlier participation as a surgeon, the teacher had introduced CPR. Today she observes without comment that CPR has become a symptom, not a treatment. She does, however, comment when Sarah seems pleased that the babies are going to die. "That would be so sad," she says, and the children pick up on her concern and devote their energies to healing. Because the children are accustomed to her involvement as a co-player, they experience her concern about the babies as that of a medical colleague or family member, rather than as an intrusive adult telling them how they're supposed to feel.

SHOPPING AT THE SUPERSTORE

The teacher at Second Street preschool loves to play with children. She is learning not to do it too much, but sometimes she joins in, as stage director and player, to encourage children to elaborate their spontaneous dramatic play. This episode begins with a discussion at group time.

TEACHER: Yesterday Yolanda and Luz were playing Shopping at the Superstore.
    I wondered if more people would like to play Shopping at the Superstore
    today? It's a big store. There's room for lots of people. What do you need to
    go shopping? Let's make a list. (*She has taped a big sheet of paper to the
    wall and writes children's suggestions on it.*)
YOLANDA: I take my purse.
LUZ: Me too.
TEACHER: You dressed up yesterday. I saw you in a purple dress.
YOLANDA: And high heels.
TEACHER: And high heels. Do men shop at the Superstore too?
LUZ: No. Only mamas.
BEN: My dad goes to the store. My mom stays home.
TEACHER: Do men work at the store?
ABDOU: They sell fish and lettuce and deli stuff. They put things in bags.
TEACHER: So we need bags in our store. What else do we need?
SARAH: Bread.
LUZ: Oranges. And milk. And fish.
TEACHER: I'm going to write "groceries." We call food at the store *groceries*.
BEN: Shopping basket.

YOLANDA: My mama buyed some dishes.

TEACHER: What did she pay for them with?

YOLANDA: The cash machine gave her money.

TEACHER: People take money to the store or they can use a cash machine there to withdraw money from the bank. Sometimes the cashier gives them change. Today I'm going to be the store manager so lots of people can play. The store will open in 5 minutes. If you want to go shopping, get dressed up. Put some money in your purse. If you want to work in the store, come help me fix it up.

Five minutes later, the teacher leads the class in a countdown: "Five, four, three, two, one . . . Store's open."

Yolanda, in high heels, purple dress, and shoulder bag, has been waiting in line, admiring the silver paper squares she has found for money. She picks up a shopping basket and goes first to a shelf where she puts dishes in her basket. Then she strolls to a table where there is a pile of plastic food. She adds some to her basket. Luz hands her an egg, which she carefully tucks in. She spends several moments trying to find a place to balance a slice of bread.

Hiking up her shoulder bag, she continues to the checkout counter, where the teacher has positioned Abdou with a supply of large paper bags. He dumps Yolanda's basket on the floor and transfers its contents, one by one, to the bag. She waits graciously.

Ben, at the cash register, is prompted by the store manager/teacher and asks, "Where's your money?" Yolanda pulls out a handful of silver, giving it to Ben. He rings it up on the cash register and gives it back.

Yolanda says "Thank you" sweetly and heads home with her bag full.

What did the children gain from the teacher's direction of their play? Their going-shopping script was expanded to include list-making, money, shopping bags, and male workers, none of which had been included in the original play. These were the teacher's ideas, intended to scaffold children's understanding of real-life props, roles, and interactions (Leong & Bodrova, 2009).

In this morning's play, she has taken the initiative away from the children. It worked, nevertheless, because this teacher is genuinely playful. She has a good sense of the children's interests and capacities and a comfortable relationship with them; they're not intimidated by her and enjoy her participation. She helps them feel important. Her involvement relieved them, for a day, of the need to spend energy on inventing a script, negotiating conflicts, and solving interpersonal problems. If she structured it this way every day, they'd miss out on a lot of important learning. She doesn't; the next day, the store play was theirs again. Several weeks later the shopping script was still being enacted at the children's initiation.

PICNIC

With a group of 3-year-olds, this teacher at Live Oak child care center feels that he is sometimes their "pied piper," and he has decided to take the lead with a new dramatic play idea and encourage the children to join him. It's his hope that the next time they'll do it themselves, freeing him to move on to the blocks or puzzles and encourage more involvement there. His presence, he has found, attracts children to wherever he is, and he uses it thoughtfully.

It's a brisk but sunny day. During snack time, the children are engaged in leisurely conversation. The teacher also uses this time to suggest choices that will be available at playtime: "I'm going to be in the playhouse area. And I'll open the back door. We haven't had a picnic for a long time. Some of the babies might like to go on a picnic—but it's pretty cold today, so they'll need clothes."

For awhile, nearly all the children are more interested in the new play dough than in a picnic. But eventually Derek remembers. He asks the teacher, and they talk about what they will need.

TEACHER: Would you like to take the blue blanket? (*He gets it.*) Now, what else are we going to need to take outside?
DEREK: Cups.
TEACHER: Cups, and . . .
DEREK: We have some cookies. We need to make them.
TEACHER: Do you remember where the cups are? (*He does. Anthony runs to join them.*) Would you like to join us on our picnic, Anthony? (*Anthony nods happily.*) What else do we need?
DEREK: A drink. Eggs. I gonna make some hard eggs.
TEACHER: Anthony, want to bring out some of the babies? (*He does.*)
DEREK: I can't find the hard eggs.

Julie has taken a broom outside; she's sweeping around the blanket, which is on the little porch outside the door.

TEACHER: Hi, Carlos. Would you like to bring your baby on the picnic, too? Do the babies need clothes?
ANTHONY and CARLOS: No. No clothes.
CARLOS: I laid my baby down.
ANTHONY: My baby's gonna sleep.
CARLOS: I gonna take my baby to the bathroom. (*He does. Derek has gone outside, leaving the pot of "hard eggs" on the stove.*)
TEACHER: It's not burning, is it? Should I go check it? (*Derek goes to check the pot on the stove.*)
DEREK (*stirring the pot*): Zoom, zoom, zoom. It's ready! It's ready! You guys share. I got some straws.

ANTHONY: I'll give me some drink of water. (*Children, babies, and teacher settle down on the blanket for a picnic.*)
JULIE: The baby's crying, guys.
CARLOS: I know.
DEREK: Baby wants eggs. Knock, knock! I gonna peel it, Baby!

Response to the teacher's picnic idea did not happen right away. Adults can afford to toss ideas out and wait to see what happens; they have lots more. Children will respond, now or later, to those ideas that make connections for them.

Picnic, a play script familiar to Derek, interested him and got him the teacher to play with. Anthony, Carlos, and Julie may have been attracted not by the prospect of a picnic but by the teacher's, or Derek's, presence in the playhouse. The back porch was a special place for friends playing picnic with babies. There are many good starting points for play.

THE FISH CAMP

Other teachers have taken a planfully active role in play with children whose traditional culture is different from that of school. The intention is to teach them the playscripts of their own culture so they will know it, and themselves, better, and to support them in the task of becoming bilingual and bicultural. This Inuk teacher, Ina Kuluguqtuq Zakal, working with Inuit children in Ottawa, intentionally guides games and involves herself in sociodramatic play to coach role-play and teach the Inuktitut language (Reynolds, 2002, pp. 98–100).

Taking the observer's hand, 4-year-old Christian guides her to a small table near a bright window. The observer is curious about this particular set of miniature figures and how a young Inuk child, growing up in the city, will play with them. Thoughtfully arranged atop a piece of caribou hide, the figures include four adults—two females and two males—with light brown skin and dark hair, sitting together inside a simple three-sided building. There are two babies in cribs. Several small dogs, a whale, a dolphin, two small tents, several coniferous trees, and several small outbuildings, and the stage is set.

Animating two adult figures, one in each hand, Christian invents the script, telling the observer, "The family is waking up and fish is for breakfast."

Ina, nearby in the art area, prompts, "Christian, what's fish in Inuktitut?"

"*Iqaluk!*" Handing a small stone to the observer, he says, "Pretend this is *iqaluk!*" With another stone, Christian and the observer invent a cooking place for the *iqaluk.* "We cut it with the knife. Cut! I cutted it. Stay there and cook, *iqaluk,*" says Christian, gesturing with a cutting motion.

Christian sets a male figure down inside the tent, and begins to snore. "Ina, Ina, what's 'daddy'?"

Ina replies, "*Ataata. Anaana* is mom."

Christian says, "*Ataata,* wake up! We have to eat *iqaluk* now!" Animating the dad figure, Christian says, "Daddy, *Ataata,* let's go walk on the ice and see fireworks! Get the dog. That's a big dog. Yahoo! Let's go!"

Ina gestures with a wave of her hand in the air, "Christian! Remember fireworks are *northern lights—ti, tu, ta!*"

Christian says, "Look at that one! A big one!" Pausing, he hands the male figure to the observer. "Now you be Daddy, and I will be Mommy."

These Inuit children, and many of their parents, are familiar and comfortable in an urban environment and Western culture. Christian's Inuk father was born in Ottawa and would prefer life in the north but considers Ottawa his home. He is less familiar with his first language of Inukti and Inuit traditions. Other families who arrived more recently from northern communities are still learning the culture of city life. This program, with its various family resources, will help them transition. All the families here want their children to learn bicultural and, eventually, bilingual competence. Some families will achieve that fine balance by learning northern ways; other families will build capacities for a Western lifestyle.

> Urban areas present special challenges for the survival of aboriginal cultures. These challenges come in part because many of the traditional sources of aboriginal culture–contact with the land, elders, aboriginal languages, and spiritual ceremonies–are difficult to maintain in cities at present. Moreover, aboriginal people are continuously exposed to perceptions, either consciously or unconsciously held, that cities are not where aboriginal cultures belong and can flourish. (Peters, 1996, p. 321)

Children and families from a cultural tradition that is different from the dominant culture base of public education need bridges to cross the gap between the two worlds successfully. Canada's aboriginal early learning programs are grounded in the philosophy that an aboriginal child's right is to have a strong personal and family identity, and to feel proud of his Native heritage and language, as the best assurance of success in kindergarten and sustained school achievement.

Through play Christian is beginning to understand the mysteries of the Inuit lifestyle, although he has not visited the North yet. Dramatic play is an important process for learning about his cultural roots, because play is a medium for inventing, communicating, and internalizing new meanings and symbols (Meier & Murrell, 1996).

WHY TEACHERS PLAY

Some teachers enter play spontaneously, for their own pleasure or the children's. They take their cues from the children, and the relationship is one of mutuality. Other teachers intentionally guide play for teaching purposes. Inherent in the role of *teacher as player* is the risk that the adult will take over, directing play that then ceases to be the children's, or will attract children looking for adult attention.

When is this risk most appropriately taken? We believe it is at beginnings, when children are still short on ideas for play in the school setting and/or skills for playing with materials and each other. There are several kinds of beginnings, including beginning child care as a young 3-year-old or entering a school culture different from one's home culture.

The Picnic sequence, like the play events with crates and cardboards described at the end of Chapter 3, involved adults in play with young 3-year-olds early in the year. Their goal was to get play started, to give children ideas and skills to be added to their repertoires. As the children became more competent players, adults were able to play and mediate less and to observe and assess in more depth.

Teachers of children who come to school unfamiliar with its materials, language, or playscripts may need to enter into play with children to build bridges from home culture to school culture. Children become competent with materials not through directed practice but through exploratory play. Very young children, learning communication skills in their home language, as well as second and third language learners, become competent with oral language through spontaneous exploration of its sounds and its possibilities for communication. They become competent with scripts of their home, neighborhood, and cultural traditions by playing them. The Inuk teacher was intentional in selecting and arranging hand-sized figures to create a miniature play world (Erikson, 1950) suggesting a fish-camp script. The child's imagined fish-camp play was the medium through which the teacher taught meaningful vocabulary and helped him complicate the story (Reynolds, 2002). Play "is not a peripheral sideline to the serious job of adults and children at school. It does not simply provide a spontaneous interlude to the more structured work of the classroom" (Sparrow, 1988, p. 234). Rather, play is basic to the early learning language program. For the young child, competence at school is learned through play.

Bridges are built from both ends. It is important that teachers also take initiative in becoming more familiar with the materials, language, and events of children's home cultures and introduce them into activities at school—not just on special occasions but as part of the daily play environment. "If I want the environment to be familiar to them, then I have to know what they are familiar with. What is the cultural context of their play? How do they use the environment? How do they interact with each other? What do I know about their culture? And lastly, have I viewed all children's play by the same standards?" (Greer Jarman, 1999, p. 54)

All children should have access to both familiar and new cultural modes; thus it is important to implement an anti-bias multicultural curriculum for the middle-class White children whose experience traditional schooling has matched most closely (Derman-Sparks & Ramsey, 2011). In doing so, teachers as well as children will find themselves challenged to learn new playscripts.

Some teachers prefer to provision the environment for changing dramatic play themes while making a conscious decision to stay out of the play themselves. "If I'm playing grocery store, children will come because I'm there," said one kindergarten teacher. "I want them to come because the play itself has meaning for them." In contrast, the teacher playing Picnic is willing to use his presence as the initial attraction for his 3-year-olds, trusting that the play will take over.

CHAPTER 5

Teacher Behavior That Interrupts Play

It is inevitable that some play will be interrupted by adults. Some interruptions are accidental; the adult wasn't playing close attention to the script. Others are intentional; the adult has a different agenda and believes it is more important than the play. Both teacher-as-mediator and teacher as player risk interrupting children's play—taking it over, or destroying it altogether for the sake of teaching something they value more. If teachers care about sustaining play, they must tailor their interventions to conform to the script the children are playing.

Children's dramatic play is a form of improvisational theater that draws its scripts from their imaginary and real-life experiences. In improvising, children often interrupt one another's scripts, which is one reason teachers are called upon as mediators. Sometimes these interruptions take place within cooperative dramatic play, when the players discover that their versions of the script differ from one another. At these points they may move out of role temporarily to argue the point; for example, "We don't need two bus drivers; no bus has two drivers!" (Smilansky & Shefatya, 1990, p. 23). Children, however, negotiate as peers, whereas if an all-knowing adult moves to set the play straight with her version of the script, she can easily take away the initiative from the children.

INTERRUPTING FOR ONE'S OWN PLEASURE IN PLAY

Adults relatively new to teaching, or reassessing their teaching, may try different approaches at different times to see what will happen. Here, for example, are two different sequences of "Kitty" play by the same children on different days. During the first, the teacher simply watched, taking notes.

Julie and Katie are in the book area, meowing. Derek comes in and says, "Here's some milk" as he puts down a green plastic saucepan.

Katie and Julie crawl to the pan and put their heads down, but Julie pushes just a little and has the pan to herself. Derek goes back to the cupboard, gets two more pans, and calls them over: "Here kitty kitty kitty, here kitty kitty." Katie and Julie crawl toward the new pans.

DEREK (to David): These are not babies. These are kittens.

ANTHONY: They need to go to the vet's. They need to go to the vet's.

DEREK: Come on, kitties. . . . I took them.

ANTHONY: They're going to the vet's. (*The children all move to the pillows in the book area.*)

DEREK: That's not cat food. Cat food has water. They have to have water. I need my fork. Open your mouth, kitty. . . . The cat has an owie. I'll take him to the vet.

ANTHONY: I'm making good food for them. They don't like that stuff. This is cake. Know what this is? Cake for them.

NICOLE: Here, kitty. (*Scooping with spoon in pan.*) Open your mouth, kitty. Now are you hungry?

ANTHONY: I need a pot. That's more. That's the same thing.

What do kitties do, and what do people do with kitties? Children who share common experiences can play Kitty, or any other script, together. These children know, collectively, that kitties drink milk and eat cat food from dishes on the floor, that they don't walk on their hind legs, and that they come when you call, "Kitty kitty kitty." Sometimes they need to go to the vet, especially if they have an owie. Feeding is a daily event in the life of cats and their people; going to the vet is a dramatic, occasional event. Children weave both the daily and the dramatic into their play; they need to understand both.

Even though Derek reminded David, "These are not babies. These are kittens," the temptation to give animals human characteristics can't be resisted altogether. "Open your mouth, kitty," say two different children, feeding kitties with a fork and spoon. And cat food—"they don't like that stuff"—is rejected in favor of cake. There are, nonetheless, clear rules to the play. On another day, when the teacher spontaneously joined in, the play was changed dramatically.

JULIE: Meow, meow.

DEREK: Woof, woof.

NICOLE: Meow, meow, meow.

LARUE (*putting on the white lab coat and the plastic safari hat*): There's my suit.

KATIE and NICOLE (*pawing at the knees of the teacher*): Meow, meow, meow. (*At this point the teacher gets down on her knees, puts her hands up as paws, and begins meowing.*)

JULIE: You can't be a cat!

TEACHER (*forlornly*): Meow.

JULIE: You're a teacher! You have to sit in that chair! (*She points to it.*)

TEACHER: But I know how to meow like a kitty.

DEREK (*pointing at David, who is lying on the floor with his eyes closed*): Uh-oh!
    The kitty died. (*The group stops and looks. No one moves or says anything.*)

TEACHER: What can we do? It's an emergency.

DEREK: I don't know.

TEACHER: We could go to the phone. Who should we call? (*There is no response.
    The children look at the teacher.*) Okay, I'll go dial 911. (*She does.*) Hello?
    Yes? We have an emergency at Live Oak Child Care Center at 1145 High
    Street. In the Sunshine Room. We have a kitty who appears to be dead!

DEREK (*putting the fire hat on his head and holding his hand with the thumb
    toward his ear*): Okay—I'm on my way. OOO OOO OOO [makes siren
    sound]. (*Children begin lying on the floor, eyes closed.*)

TEACHER: How can we help the kitties? (*Larue gets a bowl and spoon and begins
    to feed them medicine.*)

DAVID (*Jumping up*): I'm alive! I'm alive!

Others do the same. David falls back down. Another child tries to take the
bowl and spoon from Larue, who says, "No, I'm the nurse!" There are now nine
children in the house, block, and book areas, dying and reviving. Anthony comes in
and out to help.

In these children's definition of proper roles, grown-ups don't play kitty.
When the adult moved into the kitty role, the play was interrupted. She had
left the role the children had defined for her by meowing and pawing at
her–Person Who Takes Care of Kitties–to become a kitty herself. Why? As
an experiment, perhaps, to see what the children would do, or as a spontaneous bit of play on her part, because she was feeling playful. But the children
were having none of it. Children play, they remind her. Teachers take care of
children–and kitties. They don't *play* kitty.

It took Derek's and David's invention of Dead Kitty to get the play back
on track, with the teacher moving into a clearly grown-up role: helper in an
emergency. "What can we do?" she asks. They don't know. She takes over,
introducing a call-911 script, until Derek is able to plug into it by becoming
a firefighter responding to the call. Once that happens, many children are
able to collaborate in a dying, helping, and reviving script, without further
teacher intervention.

The children's temporary immobilization may have been a response to
the shock of Dead Kitty. But this was, as it turned out, a familiar dramatic

script that they all knew how to play. More shocking, perhaps, was their teacher's transformation into kitty; that wasn't in their script. The appropriate role for an adult in children's play is defined by children; they expect an adult to play their game, not her own.

These 3-year-olds were looking for a person who takes care of kitties. They were also reality-based in their distinction between children and adults and their respective places in the world: Adults are people who take care of children.

We asked another teacher at Live Oak, who spends much of her time with the 4-year-olds, "How do you play with the children?"

"Well," she said, "I taste things when they pretend to feed them to me. If they chortle, 'That's poisons,' and laugh maniacally because they've tricked me–'Ha ha, you trusted us'–I fall down dead. If they meow at me, I purr. Sometimes I initiate growling, because they like to run away scared. If they scare me, I'm properly frightened."

This is a playful young adult, but she has made a clear definition of appropriate play behaviors with children. She is willing to play victim of poisoning if older 4-year-olds, who know they're pretending, assign her that role in their play, but it isn't a role she would ever invent if they offered her pretend food. She is the gracious recipient of gifts that aren't poisoned. If they mew at her as kittens, she purrs as a mother cat. She can sometimes growl at them, as an adult bear might growl at cubs, because they have previously initiated games of scaring her and know how such games are played; as she says, "They like to run away scared."

These are all adult roles, spilling over into the sorts of games that parents play with their children and that are safe because the relationship is safe. Hiding and finding, growling and running, poisoning and reviving are all games of separation and reunion–important themes in the lives of young children. If you leave me at child care all day, do you love me? Will I be cared for? Will you come back?

This adult does not play at being a child. "If they asked me to be a baby (which they don't), I'd say, 'I don't feel like it.' It wouldn't work. The kids would get self-conscious, and the play would center around me." Children's babies, in play, can be played by dolls and each other, but not by adults.

When things are going smoothly, the natural relationship between caring adult and children is power *for*. Power exercised *for* a child means that the child is provided experiences that contribute to the development of self-esteem and confidence and thus create power for the child. From the child's point of view, the child is facilitated (Trook, 1983, in Jones & Cooper, 2006). The relationship is asymmetrical; the adult cares for the child and consciously nurtures his growth.

Sometimes the power relationship can change to a more balanced form of power-sharing, power *with*. When power is used *for* the child, the adult is intentionally guiding, structuring, or supporting toward a goal. When power *with* occurs, adult and child share a sense of wonder and are creating together. Following the child's lead in play, the adult has no agenda other than mutual interaction with the child.

The teacher playing kitty had no agenda other than mutual interaction, but she failed to follow the children's lead. Playscripts are in the children's charge; the adult player may not move beyond the script as the children define it.

Here's an example of two adults playing within the script to create power *with*.

At Madison West preschool, where today the kitchen area has been set up outdoors, Sharon and Tamara are at the stove. Laurie is by the hanging clothes, adorned in red high heels, a purple dress, and a turquoise shawl, holding a baby doll in each arm. Jorge, clad in a firefighter's suit, wheels a wooden stroller. "Look, Tamara!" he says.

Three small plastic dishes, red, yellow, and green, sit on the concrete, filled with mixtures of sand and water. Tamara scoops some from one dish to another. Laurie pours water from a tea kettle into one dish, but Tamara says, "No! Don't do that!" She looks at me and asks, "You hungry?"

I nod yes. Tamara carries over a cup, lifts the green dish, and sets them on the table I sit at. She goes back to the stove, where she sets a pot in the oven and closes the oven door. She opens it to put a lid on the pot, closes it, opens it again, and pushes in another pot.

During this time, Sharon has been washing dishes with invisible water. Now she turns to Tamara and asks, "They all clean now?" Tamara nods approval and walks to me.

TAMARA (*with a look of concern on her face*): You tell me you want some spinach?
ME: I'd love some spinach.
TAMARA: Good! 'Cause that what I made. (*She dishes some of her mind's spinach onto my plate.*)
LAURIE (*to Tamara, who is on her way back to the kitchen*): Did you put on clothes today?
TAMARA: No.
LAURIE: These are my high heels. (*She lifts one elegant foot.*)
TAMARA (*walking with Laurie to the rack where dresses are hanging*): Let me see. What kinds of dresses? Let me see, if I wear . . . should I wear this dress to the party? You want to wear this one? (*She holds out a different dress for each of them.*)

LAURIE: Oh, yes. (*She drapes the new dress around her shoulder, as a scarf for the one she's already wearing.*)

TAMARA (*with a pan in her hand, walking to the teacher*): Teacher, I brought you something.

TEACHER: What is it?

TAMARA: Spinach.

TEACHER: Spinach—mmm—would you bring me some broccoli? You know I love broccoli and mushrooms. (*Tamara runs back to the stove and fills four dishes with sand and water.*)

TAMARA (*handing the dish to the teacher*): Here's your broccoli.

TEACHER: This is broccoli? And these are mushrooms?

TAMARA: Uh-hum. (*She runs to me.*) Here's mushrooms.

ME: Umm, thank you, delicious.

(Solow, 1989, pp. 77–79)

This is play as genuine dialogue among children and between Tamara and the two adults. Both adults respond playfully and spontaneously; the teacher introduces broccoli not as new vocabulary for Tamara but because she really doesn't want spinach.

> Those rare, mutually creative interactions which are the high point of our human existence are possible only with peers. Thus it is clear that our liberation is directly related to our ability to be liberators, i.e., to help others, including children, create the power that makes them our peers as often as possible. (Trook, 1983, p. 18)

Trook's use of the word *liberation* reflects Freire's (1970) assertion that all education either domesticates or liberates. Power *with* equalizes, temporarily, the imbalance between the adult and child, making them peers in play. They both contribute good ideas, but the child retains the lead–because play is, after all, the child's world. In the play just described, the interactions are characterized by mutuality, and the child is, for the moment, no less competent than the adult.

In this episode, Tamara invited the adults to participate in her smoothly running play. When things aren't going so smoothly, responsible adults may need to intervene without being invited. Skilled mediators respond in a power *for* mode, taking the children's script seriously as they suggest alternatives for problem-solving. In contrast, adults who don't mind interrupting children's play use their power *on* children, arbitrarily replacing children's agendas with their own. Power *on* is used to domesticate, to help children learn how to behave.

INTERRUPTING TO TEACH RULES

Andy and Ruben are carefully building a platform of blocks for their cars, with an elegant double ramp leading off the platform. Ricky's fast car crashes into the ramp. Andy hits Ricky.

RICKY (*running to the assistant teacher*): Andy hit me! (*Ebony and Marina start pushing their cars down the ramp.*)
ANDY (*wailing*): No, no, no!
ASSISTANT TEACHER: Andy, come over here. You can't play if you can't share. Use your words. Don't just say No, no, no. Tell him to stop. (*Andy is silent. He looks away, toward his blocks.*) When I call you, I expect an answer. (*Andy runs back to the blocks.*)
RUBEN: Look what I'm making, guys. (*He starts to run his car on the ramp. Andy pushes Ruben's car away, and the ramp falls down.*)
ASSISTANT TEACHER: Andy, remember what we talked about. (*Andy runs to the teacher for help.*)
TEACHER (*calling from the puzzles*): Ruben, I want you and Andy to help put that bridge back together.

Ruben quietly complies. Then Andy starts building a tower; Ruben is getting blocks off the shelf for him. But the tower wobbles and falls with a crash. Ricky laughs loudly, and so does Andy. Ruben starts running a car down the ramp. Andy is rebuilding his tower, with Ricky helping him this time. This time they give it a broader base, and when it stands tall, without falling, Andy laughs loudly. Ricky echoes him.

ANDY (*exulting*): It works!
RICKY (*also delighted*): Yippee!
ASSISTANT TEACHER: Andy, do you understand? Not so loud. Use your inside voices.

Andy hit Ricky, a quick reaction, because Ricky carelessly messed up his careful construction. But Andy became the culprit because Ricky complained to the assistant teacher. Her response was power *on* moralizing: "Andy, come over here. You can't play if you can't share." Andy's concern–to protect his blocks–was ignored.

Escaping back to his play, Andy took out his frustration on Ruben's ramp, knocking it over a second time. The assistant teacher admonished Andy again, and Andy turned to the teacher–who asked Ruben to be a helpful friend. That turned out to be a power *for* intervention, because Ruben was more than willing to help. The play resumed, and Ricky got involved, too. But if Andy were a less determined block builder, the assistant teacher's interruptions to teach rules could have effectively destroyed his play, perhaps leaving Andy angrily sulking or lashing out rather than constructively engaged in play. The assistant teacher consistently ignored children's play agendas, intervening only on behalf of adult standards: "You have to share." "Use your words." "Not so loud."

Power *on* fails to help children understand their own confusing emotions and those of others. It also fails to teach children problem-solving and negotiation strategies they can use independently. Instead, it encourages immediate appeal to authority: "Teacher, he hit me." Since the adult may not have seen the sequence of events, her solutions are likely to be arbitrary, falling back on rules of behavior while ignoring the content of the play. "I'm not interested in your ramp; you have to learn to share. And when I call you, I expect an answer." Children in power *on* classrooms tattle a lot, hoping to get authority on their side first. They don't try to work things out with each other.

Power *on* is appropriate and necessary when safety is involved. It may be appropriate if the adult has a moral lesson to teach and believes it can be taught directly. But power *on* ignores and interrupts play.

Effective facilitation—power *for*—takes the script and rhythm of the play into account, even when there are conflicts to be solved.

Back at Live Oak preschool, Brad and Danny, with Matthew and Michael on the periphery, are playing a fantasy script in the roles of astronaut and crew. Their props include hollow blocks, unit blocks, trucks, small traffic signs, cars and planes, and Lincoln Logs. The dialogue is loud and fast-paced.

BRAD: Who said you could play? Nobody said you could play.

DANNY: I'm the chief astronaut.

BRAD: No, I'm a astronaut.

DANNY: I said it first!

BRAD: I'm telling. Teacher, teacher! He said he's gonna take my spot.

TEACHER: You know, on every space shuttle mission there are 8 or 9 astronauts.
     Are you the crew in charge of computers?

BRAD: I'm the astronaut.

DANNY: Can I be chief astronaut, and you be the computer astronaut?

BRAD: Sure. I'm a computer guy. You're not. You're Captain Astronaut.

DANNY: Sorry sorry sorry sorry sorry. Come on, man.

BRAD: Want to get the computer? Space shuttle computer.

DANNY: Mine goes like that. Hold it, man.

Working together—Michael and Matthew are actively helping now—the boys gradually construct an identifiable vehicle out of a line of blocks—it turns out to be the space shuttle. "Fuel" and "dehydrated potatoes" made of Lincoln Logs are inserted into the hollow at the rear.

MICHAEL: Where do I sit? We gonna blast off?
BRAD: No, no! That's my smoke thing. There's fire in there, see? This is going to be the smoke thing. Danny, Danny. Put it right here. Hammer it.
MICHAEL: It'll burn you.
DANNY: He's our friend. Let him on. (*Matthew has arrived. He sits down.*)
MICHAEL: That's gonna burn you!
MATTHEW (*hastily standing up*): Ow!

Zach and Warren arrive. They try to sit down. Michael tells them there's an explosion, to get out, and they appeal to the teacher. "That's hot there, I think it's exploding on liftoff, watch out," she says.

MICHAEL: *Challenger's* gonna explode. Get out!
DANNY: It's fire! And smoke. Jump off!

All six boys roll off the blocks and crash out onto the ground, yelling "Woowee!" "Yikes!" "Scary!" "Hot smoke!"

This teacher's words connect children with the rules of the playscript rather than the rules of the classroom, encouraging them to devise solutions for themselves. If you pay attention, maybe you can find a place in the space shuttle script. "That's hot there, watch out!" "Are you the crew in charge of computers?" in response to "Teacher, teacher! He said he's gonna take my spot," reminds the player of his role rather than trying to solve the dispute. The adult facilitator takes the playscript seriously; she helps the children sustain and enrich it with her comment, "I think it's exploding on liftoff, watch out."

INTERRUPTING TO TEACH CONCEPTS

The interruption of play also happens in the name of cognitive stimulation; the teacher intervenes to teach vocabulary and concepts. Adults who have learned that play should be taken seriously sometimes try to adapt it to their own idea of what's serious.

At Second Street child care center, Ebony is playing in the block area as her teacher watches.

EBONY: Watch this. (*She rolls a car down the ramp.*)
TEACHER: Ebony, is that the freeway?
EBONY: Yeah. Watch this, teacher!
TEACHER: Is your car going down? Is it going down the freeway ramp? Is it going fast? How many cars do you have? Is your car going up again? Ebony, can you answer my question?

No, Ebony isn't interested in the teacher's questions. She is absorbed in her play, until Marina grabs the ramp. Ebony squeals.

TEACHER: Marina, Ebony had it first. You drive your car there. It needs to go in the same direction. (*Marina tentatively pushes her car down the ramp after Ebony's car. Ebony doesn't mind.*)
MARINA: Look at me. Look at me. Look at my car. (*No one responds.*)

These are young 3-year-olds. The adult's intent was to stimulate more complex language, but, as often happens, the adult's language was all that could be heard. After asking, "Ebony, is that the freeway?" she asked five more questions in rapid succession, introducing *up* and *down, freeway* and *ramp*, and *how many*, all at once. "Ebony, can you answer my question?" she finally insisted. No way. Ebony's interest was in her car—"Watch this"—not in answering questions, and the teacher's intended facilitation fell flat. The teacher thought she was using power *for*, but power is defined by its outcomes, rather than its intent. It is defined from the child's point of view.

Perhaps Ebony just didn't want to talk. But she had initiated the conversation with "Watch this." Here are some possible alternative dialogues.

EBONY: Watch this.
TEACHER: Ebony, is that the freeway?
EBONY: Yeah. Watch this.
TEACHER: I'm watching. It goes fast, doesn't it?
EBONY: Yeah. It go real real fast. Want to watch it again?
TEACHER: Can you make it go faster?
EBONY: Yeah. Real real fast. Lookit! I pushed it HARD.

EBONY: Watch this.
TEACHER: Ebony, is that the freeway?
EBONY: Yeah. Watch this.
TEACHER: Your car is going down the freeway.
EBONY: My car is going fast down the freeway. There it go!
TEACHER: It's going really fast. That's a fast car.
EBONY: That my fast car.

In both these dialogues the teacher experiments with descriptions of the car and its action. In each, Ebony expands her vocabulary in response to the teacher's suggestions, which are offered within Ebony's own agenda—"Watch!"—and respond to the action of the moment: The car is going fast.

This teacher is eager to think about her interactions with children; she was actively interested in the alternative dialogues that the observer suggested.

"Come again, won't you?" she asks, "And bring the video camera. If we have a video, we can watch it together later."

When the day scheduled for videotaping arrives, she has decided to use block play again, this time with dinosaurs and zoo animals, as the setting for teaching "position words"–*under* and *over*, *top* and *bottom* and *side*–in support of the lesson she has planned for that day.

TEACHER: What could we do with them? He's got a long neck.
VICTOR: Look at my long one.
TEACHER: Does that one fit under the bridge? . . . Look at Jerry, he's got his
    dinosaur on top of his head. Let's see if I can put mine on top of my head.
    Look, it fell down.
JERRY: You can't reach my dinosaur.
TEACHER: I can't reach your dinosaur. Let me try. . . . The cow is inside of the bus.
    . . . He's driving on top of my legs. Want me to make a bridge with my legs?
    Then he can go underneath my legs.
ANNIE: He's going to jail.
TEACHER: Why?
ANNIE: Because he been bad. (*Victor zooms along with a speeding fire truck.*
    Several children join the firefighter theme.)
TEACHER: What is that car doing there? Looks as if it's riding on top of my knee.

Later the teacher and observer watch the video together and talk about it. "I had in my plans to teach position words, so that's what I did in the block area. I think maybe I used too many, though; one or two would have been enough," the teacher reflects.

The observer responds, "I could hear you 'underlining' them as you said them. I was interested to see how your plan gave you the reason to be in the blocks and stay there. The children liked having you there. The video shows, though, that sometimes your words prompted not sustained play but 'Look at me, teacher.' Putting dinosaurs on top of heads was fun, but it didn't take the play anywhere. Look, there's Jerry putting it back on his head and asking you to look at him. He's more interested in your attention than in playing."

The teacher agrees. "But what about my lesson?" she asks. The observer asks, "Could you keep it in mind and look for opportunities to use position words in context? When Annie drove her plane up to the block arch, your spontaneous question, 'Will it go under the bridge?' was her question, too, and you put it in words for her. At that moment, *under* was part of the play sequence; it was language in context."

The teacher laughs, "Oh, and that's what was happening at snack time. We had fruit cocktail, and the children started looking for the grapes. I remembered to bring in position words: 'Where was your grape? Was it at the bottom?'"

The observer says, "And the children used the words, too, because the position of the grapes was part of the game. In the block play, you used position words but the children didn't. Drama was their agenda: dinosaurs, and jail, and fire truck, not inside and down."

Lesson plan outcomes that are as specific as this one are apt to lead teachers into inappropriate behavior. If objectives must be written, the adult can try for something like, "Children will communicate needs, thoughts, and ideas during play." Such general objectives alert teachers to observe children's behavior while retaining role options for themselves (Gronlund, 2006). If children are talking as they play, the teacher can watch and listen without intervening. If they aren't talking, or if their vocabulary is monotonous, she might decide to enter into the action to complicate it and to encourage verbalization. Adult intervention in play should be designed to sustain it, not get it off track.

BUILDING ON CHILDREN'S PLAY

Attentive teachers building on play are "engaging the minds of young children," in Katz and Chard's words (2000, p. 159). Some teacher guidance during play can be preplanned, as in Shopping at the Superstore (Chapter 4). At other times it comes out of on-the-spot judgments made by the teacher as mediator, as in the discussion of knives with the Ninja Turtles in Chapter 3, and in the following episode:

> On a day when the 4-year-old boys were suddenly running around the yard and through the house in wild, delightfully silly pursuit, seemingly oblivious to other children, doors, or the clatter they were generating, I stopped them after about five minutes. Since their rambling had not developed naturally into something with more of a purpose, I suggested they make a plan for their play.
>
> Geoffrey called it "Flight of the Rambos." I don't know if he had the idea before the running or as a result of it. To help them develop the context for this theme, I urged that we decide on a few rules for their play. The cardboard tubes they had were to be telescopes. And they wanted to build flying ships for themselves out of large hollow blocks. I asked several other questions, to help develop their thinking. What is the design for the flying ships? Will you need supplies for them? Who will play the navigator, and who will be the co-pilots? (Reynolds, 1988, pp. 88–89)

For two of the boys, this was an interruption; they left the play. For the rest, it was a welcome challenge to their competence in building, inventing, playing roles, and cooperating.

> Geoffrey was doing a lot of verbal planning and cooperating, which was new for him. Ty gave up needing to be in control and engaged in mutual problem-solving. Fredy found the play to be so stimulating and fulfilling that he no longer needed to be silly. None of the children was excluded, and Brian was easily accepted in the role he had created for himself as a neighboring flyer.
>
> What delighted me was that after my initial assertion for a theme and some rules, the boys took over. They directed the entire scenario. (Reynolds, 1988, p. 89)

"The boys took over" is the criterion for the success of this intervention; it focused and extended, not destroyed, the play. In play, the children are in charge. Appropriate teacher intervention is open-ended, leaving the choice with the children. Play is always negotiable; adults set the limits within which it occurs, but children invent the play itself and the changing rules that govern it.

When in doubt, trust the play. It is the children's curriculum. Play that is scattered or potentially disruptive may require refocusing, but well-focused, complex play requires no intervention. It has its own rhythm and will come to its own conclusion. It takes place on the children's turf, on which the adult has no legitimate role.

Adults who interrupt play, whatever their reasons, are usually in so much of a hurry that they fail to pay attention to children's purposes. SLOW DOWN is advice to keep in mind. We shortchange young children when we hurry them. We learn most about them, and help them learn most, when we pay attention to what is happening for them as they play.

CHAPTER 6

Teacher
as Scribe

Many adults are helped to pay attention if they have a defined task that keeps their attention focused. Some teachers of young children spent their practice teaching days with a pad and pencil in a pocket, ready to take anecdotal notes on children's behavior and turn them in to a supervisor or discuss them at a seminar. Some of them keep this habit throughout their careers. Carol fits observation and note-taking into every day.

When I observe, that's all I do. I have a piece of paper and write down little ideas and notes. It's interesting because when I do that, the children will often come over and want me to write something down or draw something. I think there needs to be a balance of being in the play and interacting with children but also being able to pull back, and just watch. It's not that I am doing nothing. If we're constantly chatting and talking with children, we're missing out on some key experiences in their play.

(Carol Sowa, teacher)

Other teachers simply give up note-taking. What would they do with all those notes if they kept on taking them? In this chapter and the next two, we suggest reasons for continued note-taking and for making other representations of children's play. These activities emphasize the teacher as collector and organizer of data—solid professional behaviors that challenge teachers' skills and encourage them to pay close attention to the content of children's play. One role that requires these behaviors is teacher as scribe.

In times before writing was a tool used by people in their daily tasks and routines, communities had professional scribes, playwrights, draftsmen, and sculptors to record and communicate news, events, myths, designs, lineage, wills, acts of gods and kings, and prayers. In early learning communities, most children do not use writing regularly; they're just beginning to learn about the process and the mechanics. The adults in the group, who all day long have endless reasons to write, are modeling the writing process. They are the community scribes.

Literacy and mathematics learning is the central focus of primary grades curriculum. Speaking, writing, reading, and math calculations are tools the mind uses for representing and communicating human experience. Dramatic play is young children's mode of representing their experience; they are pretending to be and do many things. They play at "nurturing and guiding like a daddy or a mommy, presenting a story like a reader, planning and building carefully like a worker, taking the time to think and write a list like a shopper, sitting with your family like a newspaper reader, or acting with care and courage like a fire fighter" (Stadler, 1990, p. 42). They are representing their observations of adult behavior in their play.

Pretend play is practice in meaning-making that culminates in literacy, the most abstract form of representation (Vygotsky, 1978). Gesture (bye-bye, peek-a-boo), playing with sounds, and spoken language, which young children are rapidly mastering, are forms the young child uses to represent what she knows and to communicate with others. Children represent their thinking in two- and three-dimensional constructions, paintings of monsters, drawings of family, snakes of play dough, and roads of blocks. Many children recognize their names and friends' names in print. They love to point out letters they know, and they even write them, or pretend-write them.

REPRESENTING CHILDREN'S PLAY

Teachers observing children's play often write notes describing what they see, along with taking a photo or two that captures the action, to be used in their developmental summaries, meetings with parents, and curriculum planning. These notes serve as communication to adults. Teachers can also use representations, both written and pictorial, of children's play and language to communicate with the children.

Kelly is building a tower of large colored plastic blocks. In his second year of preschool at Jefferson East, Kelly is learning to focus on a task and make friends. Kelly is very interested in printed words, and he is comfortable with adults. Kelly loves building with blocks, but his challenge is to construct stable block towers—they are apt to tumble over. How could an adult help him focus on this task?

As Kelly builds, an observer tries drawing his tower on the nearby chalkboard. He is instantly alert. "What are you doing?" "I'm drawing your tower," answers the observer (see Figure 6.1a). "That's not right," insists Kelly, "they're a circle." The observer erases her rectangles and tries again, "Like this?" (See Figure 6.1b.) Kelly is critical. "No!" (But clearly he's interested in the challenge: How do you draw a cylinder?) The observer tries again: "Is this okay?" (See Figure 6.1c.) Yes, that will do.

FIGURE 6.1. "Kelly made that blocks."

Kelly keeps building. The observer keeps drawing. They admire each other's work. She writes, "Kelly built a building." Kelly tries to read it: "Kelly made that blocks." She crosses out "built a building" and writes his words. Kelly points, "That's the top of it. This is the floor." She writes his words (see Figure 6.1d).

Kelly does some more building, including a row of triangles, which the observer draws (see Figure 6.1e). Without noticing the drawing, he runs over to the play dough. Julio takes over the chalk and chalkboard for the next 15 minutes, but he doesn't erase the triangles. Ten minutes later Kelly glances over. "Hey! He drew my triangles!"

A week later when the observer returns, Julio is building a tower with many of the same blocks. Again the observer tries drawing it—on paper this time, because the block-builders are in front of the chalkboard. She draws the outline with a marker and then decides to use crayons to color the blocks to match Julio's.

And here is Susana, wanting paper too. Susana draws Julio's tower, recognizably. She shows it to the observer, who asks, "Do you want to color it?" Yes, she does, and the observer gets crayons and more paper for Susana and for two other girls who want to draw too. Susana shows her colored drawing to the observer. "Do you want to write your name?" the observer asks. Yes, she does, with a string of letters along the bottom of the page.

Julio has enlisted help from Sandra, the teacher, to steady his tall, tall tower. He's standing on a chair to build it higher. DOWN it falls. Sandra sympathizes and invites him to build it again. She shows him the drawing of it that the observer has laid on the floor nearby.

At first he doesn't recognize it. Then, suddenly, he gets it. He takes it and holds it up to show the other block-builders. "Look, guys! It's my tower. Build it like this." They get to work, and he puts the drawing down to join them. The observer and the teacher exchange delighted glances. "May I tape it up here?" asks the observer. She puts it on the wall.

Susana has been busy drawing. She has drawn the tower twice more, on new sheets of paper, and again written her "name" along the bottom. The observer tapes up her drawings, too.

Just as children can discover that their words, spoken, make print, Julio has discovered that his block-building can make a drawing, and that a drawing can be a design for another builder to follow. That's a good thing to know. Meanwhile, Susana has observed the observer-as-scribe and tries on this role for herself, effectively and with concentration. Playing-at-being-an-adult-who-writes (or draws) is an absorbing activity for many children. It is helpful to children to offer them models of adults in this kind of action.

SHARING REPRESENTATIONS WITH CHILDREN

It doesn't take much drawing skill to sketch a block tower. But Theresa, another teacher, has real drawing skill and likes to use it, as part of her own playfulness in teaching. One day she made this observation in her preschool classroom.

In the house area a group of children gathered using the telephones. Rosa was talking to the doctor: "Doctor, *mi niña está muy enferma.*"

On the side of the house area were Juan, Joanie, Yolanda, Alex, and Diana. They had dressed up with clothes from the house area and sat in a row of chairs, one in back of the other. Yolanda was driving the "train." There were plastic crates that were hauled from the block area; Yolanda put all her belongings in the crates, and then all the other children on the train did, too.

The children played for about 15 minutes. Then suddenly they all dispersed to different areas. It was interesting to see how they carried on without an adult.

(Theresa Barrios, teacher observer)

Theresa drew the picture in Figure 6.2 to go with her written observation, sketching it quickly and then finishing it after school. The next day she brought it to circle time. "Do you know what I saw yesterday?" she asked the children. "I saw Rosa talking to the doctor on the telephone. 'My baby is very sick,' she told the doctor. And I drew a picture of her. Do you see her?" Theresa held up the picture and the children squeezed close to see. "Rosa," they said. *"Con el teléfono."* Rosa, overwhelmed, put her hands over her face. Yolanda, who had been looking closely at the picture, burst out, "That's me! I driving!"

"Yes, that's Yolanda," agreed the teacher. "Yolanda and Juan and Diana and Alex and Joanie went on the train. And here they are." There was great excitement. Our teacher drew our picture, and there we are!

At the end of circle time there was a rush for the crates and chairs. Reminding children of their interesting play encourages them to replay it, to understand and elaborate it more fully.

Young children in a group can talk, briefly, about what they've been playing, but their talk generally lacks the richness of detail that characterized the

FIGURE 6.2. "Mi niña está muy enferma."

play itself. And children find it hard to listen to each other in a large group; the teacher is more practiced in holding the attention of an audience. By using her own representations of children's play, she can stimulate children's oral language as well as their understanding that play can be represented on paper. This teacher is indeed teaching, while acknowledging the importance of the children's play and deriving her teaching directly from it. Children are most likely to understand representation when it mirrors their own actions.

Group meetings and conversations that reflect on a morning's play can be used intentionally for teaching purposes when they are play-based, not didactic (Miller & Almon, 2009). But if you're 4 or 5, self-directed imaginary and sociodramatic play is a more cognitively challenging task. Group discussions require active teacher scaffolding and reduce the time children could be playing. Good play is organically scaffolded–the challenge of the rules of play nurtures children's ability to behave "a head taller" than themselves (Vygotsky, 1978).

Today the observer who likes drawing block buildings is at Second Street School with the 4-year-olds. A good many children are absent because of flu, and the teacher is more available to individual children than she is often able to be. She is helping Edward and Richard build a structure with the hollow blocks and boards; it's as tall as her head, but she's keeping it safe.

"It's a Totally Hidden Video," says Edward, explaining and demonstrating how it works. The holes in the blocks, all lined up, are just right for looking through a camera. Edward takes his teacher's picture ("ch ch ch ch ch" says the camera), and Katie's too, when she comes over from the art table to see what's going on.

"Do you have a real camera?" the observer asks the teacher. "That's an amazing structure."

"No," the teacher apologizes. "We loaned it to the toddler program for a few days."

"Maybe I'll draw it, then," says the observer, secretly delighted. Drawing offers more possibilities. She makes one, and writes a description on it. At clean-up time, when Richard is putting blocks away, the teacher says to him, "Richard, don't take the camera down. Leave the camera up. We would like to take a picture of everyone."

The children have come together on the rug, where the teacher invites them to talk about their morning and writes their words with a marker. A teaching assistant tacks them up on a bulletin board so everyone can see (see Figure 6.3).

It's Edward's turn to talk about his video camera. He demonstrates it. Then the observer is invited to share her drawing (see Figure 6.4). She does, reading the words. Edward looks at the picture critically: "This one isn't here." He points to the tall block at the upper right. "You're right," says the observer. "I drew it and then you changed it. You know what I'll do? I'll change the picture. I'll cross out that block, like this." And she does.

FIGURE 6.3. "What we played this morning."

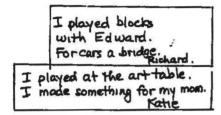

> I played blocks
> with Edward.
> For cars a bridge.
> Richard.
> I played at the art table.
> I made something for my mom.
> Katie

> I played in the art area.
> I colored. I played with
> animals.
> Katie wanted to play animals.
> And Richard. Then Mrs.
> Kelly made a butterfly and
> he got big. Stephanie

They count the blocks across the top of the drawing to see if it's accurate now. Touching each block one time as he counts by rote, Edward counts, "One, two, three, four, five. Five!"

Edward points to three more blocks in the picture that were removed from the structure during clean-up. The observer crosses them out, too. The observer asks, "So, if one block was removed from the top row, and three more big ones from the bottom row, how many blocks total is that?" This time Edward does not need to count manually. Taking a quick look to eyeball the crossed-out blocks, he knows the answer: "Four!"

"Good counting. High five!" says the teacher.

FIGURE 6.4. "A totally hidden video."

> Edward and Richard
> and Mrs. Scott made
> a Totally Hidden
> Video.
> "This is the picture,"
> said Edward.
> "It takes pictures
> by itself."

Edward has not only represented an idea he had; the observer has reproduced his representation in another medium, the picture, and he has "read" it accurately. A thoroughly impressive accomplishment when one is 4 years old. Guided by the observer, who sees the potential for learning math, he has also practiced quantifying small sets of blocks and addition skills (Sarama & Clements, 2009). Edward receives the offer to count crossed-out blocks as power *for,* and his interest in using mathematical language to describe the camera's changes pleases the observer.

Drawing, writing, and counting are forms of representation that allow teachers to model behaviors children can do. Simple, clear drawings invite children to compare them with the original, to read the diagram, and to draw for themselves. Pictures in any mode encourage reflection on experience. In her classroom Deb photographs toddlers' explorations of materials and uploads the photos onto a computer. As they engage with flubber (or paint and clay), seeing themselves and their most recent work on the computer nearby encourages interactions and their understanding of process (Curtis & Carter, 2008). Children's minds meet when an experience they've shared is reflected in images.

Wendy uses photos to create homemade books the infants love to carry around and look at again and again. The words from this one about infants' sensory play are sublime.

Foot painting
Slippery paint
Careful
Colours
Flour is soft
Pouring water
Slippery oil
Painting with fingers
Blowing bubbles
Catch them
Down

(Wendy Nethercote, teacher)

STIMULATING WRITING AS PLAY AND COMMUNICATION

There is also the written word, to be shared by adults and child writers. On another day at Second Street, an observer who sits down at the outside table with her pen and yellow pad finds herself surrounded by eager future writers.

STEPHANIE: I want to help you. What are you doing?
OBSERVER: I'm writing about children playing.
STEPHANIE: Could I have some of your paper, please? (*The observer gives her a sheet of paper and a pen.*) I'm going to write about children playing, too.

Soon there are five children writing (the observer is relieved to find an accumulation of pens at the bottom of her bag). One makes very accurate letters; one invents cursive script. All seriously tackle the task in their own ways. They are disappointed when it's time to go inside.

Returning the next week, the observer brings along a writing toolbox to be shared. Stocked with paper, recycled envelopes, pens and pencils, staplers, tape, and scissors, it enjoys instant popularity. Six children are already engrossed in creating with the materials when the teacher comes over with a crying Richard. He is sad about his mother's departure and has been crying for some minutes.

The teacher invites him to join in the activity: "Here's some yellow paper. Write Mommy a note and tell her you miss her." Pointing to the container, she asks, "Would you like to choose a pen?" Then, "We'll give Mommy the note when she comes to pick you up this afternoon."

Literacy gives power. Richard stops crying immediately, though he continues to look sad. He clutches the pen high above the point, making letters and letter-like forms. The teacher sits close to him.

When he has stopped writing, she asks, "Richard, do you want to tell me about this?" Richard doesn't respond, so she continues, "Want me to write something down?" She waits a bit, but he is still silent. "Is this to Mommy? Want me to write that down?" Richard nods, and the teacher writes, "To Mommy." "What else do you want to say?" she asks. When no response is forthcoming, she suggests, "Want to think about it?"

She gives the pen back to him, and he writes a bit more. Then, in a quiet voice, he starts speaking to the observer seated across the table from him:

"I got a balloon at my house.
"The air is coming out.
"It's blue.
"While I was asleep.
"While I was eating cereal. Oatmeal cereal.
"I have apples at my house. And oranges.
"My house is blue.
"And pears."

He shows the observer two tiny, recognizable drawings he has made with the pen on a large sheet of paper: "That's my pear right here. And this is my apple."

Again, the children are playing at being writers, enjoying the power that it gives them to be like, and to communicate with, adults—even absent mommies. It is the action of writing, not the product, that is important, though Stephanie shows the observer her carefully printed "LOVE" and Richard, after leaving the table, comes back to get his letter to Mommy and put it safely in his cubby. Adults, who have mastered writing, may choose from time to time to revisit writing products with children to remember words they have said and plans they have made, in the process also demonstrating that writing is talking written down.

WRITING CAN BE READ

At Jefferson East preschool, having just finished reading the children a book about marine animals, Irma, the teaching assistant, tells them they can look at it during free play. Now the children are planning together before they go off to play, in two groups, with the teacher and the teaching assistant. The adults have big sheets of paper and markers.

TEACHER: I'm going to write a name. *(She writes "Barbara.")*
BARBARA *(recognizing her name)*: Irma's book.
TEACHER *(writing)*: Barbara—look at Irma's book. *(Continuing to the next child.)* Luis.
LUIS *(recognizing his name)*: En la cocina—con comida.
KELLY: That's not *my* name. What's *cocina*?
TEACHER: A kitchen. *(She continues writing the children's names and choices.)*
KELLY: In the playhouse.
TEACHER: Do you know what you're going to do in the playhouse? Have you decided?
KELLY: I'm gonna cook. *(The teacher writes his words.)*
SUSANA: A jugar con los bloques de colores.
KELLY: What is *colores*?
TEACHER: *Colores* is colors.

The list is complete. As the teacher reads it aloud, the children move off to their play—except for Luis and Karl, who are more interested in the planning list. Luis, who is 5 years old and can write his name, uses the teacher's marker to add writing of his own to the list and to circle some letters and words. When he's finished, the teacher asks him to take it to the art table, where she invites Karl to have a turn. Karl spontaneously practices circling words at random, making circles, and drawing on his hand. Learning to write takes lots of practice, of many kinds.

After clean-up time the children join Irma on the rug as they're ready. The teacher arrives with the planning lists, which she puts on the floor in front of her. The children are a close, interested group as she reads down the list. "Did you play with the blocks, Susana?" she asks. "Did you play with the train, Julio? No? Okay."

It is clear to the children that this is functional print; it gives the teacher messages. Some of them are looking at her; some of them are looking at the print themselves, finding their names and their friends'.

Later, when the children are outdoors, Kelly comes over to Irma to show her his sand pie, neat in its shiny pie pan. The teacher, nearby, writes down his words as he speaks (see Figure 6.5). Kelly turns and sees the big sheet of paper with his name on it. "What's that?" he asks, to which the teacher responds, "Can you read that?" "Yes," he says, "Kelly." She reads the rest to him, pointing out the words. When she reads "three cherries," he says, "Four cherries."

(Sandra Rangel, teacher/observer)

In this preschool Kelly and Luis, among the oldest children, are actively interested in written words. Dianna, who teaches kindergarten, enjoys scribing children's words and reading them back. Dianna tells this story (Ballesteros, 1988):

One day we offered bubbles as a choice at the back table. When the six children choosing that center arrived to play, conversation burst (and we wrote down their words).

You can stack them.
The bubbles.
You can build with them.
Put one of yours on top of mine.
On the table.
See they stick together. Yours is bigger.
We made a bubble cave.
I have a tiny bubble.
I have a row of bubbles.
One big bubble. Double bubble.

FIGURE 6.5. "Four cherries."

Kelly said, "Irma, I made a pie.
Cherry pie.
One cherry.
Two cherries.
Three cherries
Four cherries."

She's got a triple.
Oh oh. Ooooh!
How did you do that?
Can we take them home?

At group time, these words-written-down are introduced by the teacher to the children; "Did you know you made a bubble poem?" She reads it to them. Then she writes, "Bubbles, Bubbles, Bubbles" at the top and asks, "Do you know what this word says?"

"Bubbles!" "Do you see the word 'bubbles' anywhere else on the page? Would someone like to come up here and take a crayon and make a circle—a bubble!—around one of the bubble words?"

Here's an exciting challenge for some of the children, and plenty of turns. (You can put more than one circle around a word, they decide.) Then they read it again, the teacher pointing to the words so everyone can shout "bubble!" each time they get to one.

The bubble poem stays up on the wall, where children can look at it as they choose. The next day they read it together again. "Who was playing with the bubbles?" asks the teacher, and she writes down the names of the six children as they identify themselves. "Now, see if you can remember one thing you said about the bubbles. Caitlin?"

Caitlin wants more time to think. Virgil volunteers. "The bubbles."
The teacher writes: "Virgil said, 'The bubbles.'"
Cassandra: I love bubbles.

Those words don't seem to be in the poem, but that doesn't matter, and the teacher doesn't mention it. They're Cassandra's words, and the teacher writes them. Pretty soon she has written the phrases shown in Figure 6.6.

FIGURE 6.6. "Bubbles, bubbles, bubbles."

Virgil said, "The bubbles."
Cassandra said, "I love bubbles."
Lizzy said, "Double bubble."
Caitlin said, "Triple bubble."
Rafael said, "We made a bubble cave."
Jorge said, "I love bubbles."
We all said, "Bubbles, bubbles, bubbles."

This teacher as scribe is building serious reading lessons on the active play of 5-year-olds. "Bubbles" is a word both memorable in experience and distinct in its shape as a word. Wetly real bubbles will continue to be available in the classroom, as will the word that represents them. And the children will keep learning both about the properties of bubbles and about the properties of words.

As children gain mastery of play, the role of teacher as scribe becomes more appropriate than the role of teacher as player. Children's capacity for dramatic play is accompanied by increasing capacity for representational drawing and construction, and interest in the modes of representation, including writing, used by adults. Scribed representations of children's play can stimulate a debriefing process in which children and adults encounter one another on the shared turf of mutual curiosity. What happened? Let's remember it, and look at it, and talk about it.

CHAPTER 7

Teacher
as Assessor
and Communicator

Teachers are responsible for teaching. They are also responsible for assessing children's learning and development and communicating their assessments to children, families, and principals or supervisors. Developmentally appropriate assessment relies on observations of children's behavior made by the people who know them best in this setting, their teachers. Ongoing observations provide a much more adequate sample of behavior than any test for young children. They permit focus on children's *abilities*, not weaknesses—what the child can and does do, rather than on what she has not yet mastered.

How do teachers know what to observe? They try to look for individual children's strengths—both interests and skills, since skill learning comes out of the pursuit of interests—and to systematize observations over time so no child is missed. There may be more notes for some children than others, but there are records for each child, extending over time and mapping growth in all its variability. Records include teacher representations—photographs, drawings, and written words—of children's play, language, and constructions with nonexpendable materials (Kuschner, 1989; New, 1990), as well as samples of children's work—paintings, drawings, and writing. For example, one kindergarten teacher (Meade-Roberts, 1988) includes in each child's portfolio a monthly sample of the roll sheet on which she asks the children to sign in every morning. This enables her to see the successive approximations of their names, as in the development of Marco's "signature":

September: ⋀⋁

November: M◊

March: MAЯCО

ASSESSMENT AS PART OF PLANNING

The No Child Left Behind (NCLB) Act of 2001 offers federal funding to schools at all levels, based on accountability for children's achievement levels. The NCLB's image of teaching is a technical transmission model: What teachers do and say is scripted; they have no control over testing practices, and they have little autonomy in deciding curriculum content (Cochran-Smith & Lytle, 2006). As this emphasis has become paramount everywhere, most states are adopting child outcome standards for the many settings that serve preschool-age children. Understandably, supervisors may be caught in the accountability web, expecting teachers to "teach to the test"–to design their curriculum as cramming for exams.

Assessment is indeed an essential part of curriculum planning. To be an integral part of the planning process, assessment must be designed by teachers themselves to contribute to their knowledge of each child's growth in understanding. Goal setting, a dynamic process continually adjusted by teachers in each program, should be developmentally appropriate, including attitudes and dispositions as well as knowledge and skills, physical and social-emotional as well as cognitive development (Bodrova, Leong, & Shore, 2004; Katz, 2008; National Association for the Education of Young Children, 2003). A child's knowledge of shapes, colors, numbers, and letters–standard kindergarten fare–is not the only indicator of school readiness (Elkind, 2008b). Informal and systematic observation during independent activity, including play, is the developmentally appropriate assessment tool in early childhood education.

Among one teacher's goals for her 5-year-olds is the acquisition of fine motor skills. She observes systematically during free play.

> Each day we note a child's approach to tasks and his first choice of activity. For many weeks I noticed that Adrian never chose to work with scissors, crayons, or markers. The drawings in his journal were lightly marked, random crayonings. It was becoming clear to me that Adrian needed to practice doing some of the things he steered clear of. Since Rosa Linda, with whom I co-teach, and I agreed that Adrian needed to be taught to cut, she sat with him one morning, and without passing judgment because he couldn't use scissors, she showed him how. After that he practiced whenever he chose to; I never singled him out again for "cutting." By the year's end Adrian could cut, usually quite accurately. (Meade-Roberts, 1988, p. 96)

The teacher is able to observe Adrian's fine motor skills, as well as his skills in building with blocks, making friends, and using language to meet his needs, because she has set the stage. As the basic elements in her curriculum, she (1) provides a physical environment full of many different things appropriate for 5-year-olds to do, (2) offers choices among all those different things, and (3) schedules the day for extended periods of choice. By giving Adrian permission to play, she has freed herself to observe him. Observing, she values the choices he makes and is able to note both his strengths and the areas in which she may need to challenge him.

Teachers also plan challenges for small groups of children. Playtime is balanced by what is called "committee time" in some programs, 20 to 30 minutes during which a heterogeneous, continuing small group of children "is given a task to do within the confines of one learning center. There are many activities planned that cover a wide ability range, and the children use materials that are open-ended (blocks, for example). It is hoped that they will learn to work with one another, depend on one another and help one another in a small group setting" (Stritzel, 1989, pp. 24–25). The teacher chooses these activities based on his observations of children at play; having assigned them, he can interact or observe in any of the same roles he adopts during playtime.

When teachers are free to choose where to begin observing, they often begin, sensibly, with children whose behavior challenges adults and sometimes other children, the non-thrivers (Prescott, Jones, Kritchevsky, Milich, & Haselhoef, 1975). Their implicit question is, What can I do to support this child in school?

CAN I LEARN TO APPRECIATE THIS CHILD MORE?

One of the teachers at Second Street preschool told us that she looks for opportunities to free herself to observe one child's behavior, in order to get to know him better. Occasionally there is help from a parent volunteer. And there are times of the day when numbers are reduced: morning arrival, late afternoon, and during wakers (children who wake first get up to play quietly at several activity centers). If there's a child she's having difficulty with, she explains, that may determine her focus, as it did one morning.

Jimmy and Thomas have not settled into school and our routines; they've been driving us crazy with their out-of-bounds behavior at group and clean-up times. I think I've tried every behavior guidance strategy in the book! This morning, when his father dropped him off, Jimmy tried running out the door after him. I held Jimmy's hand and brought him back into the classroom, but he angrily pushed several puzzles off a table. I was firm in following through, and he did help me pick everything up, sort of. Then he sat sucking his thumb. I had been intending to observe him, but I was feeling pretty frustrated, so I began watching Thomas instead. But it wasn't long before I was observing Jimmy, too. Here's what I recorded in my jot notes.

8:55 Thomas has been wandering for 5 minutes. Now he disappears out of my line of sight into the book corner behind the bookshelf.

9:05 Thomas does not reappear for 5 minutes! I peek into the corner to see what he's up to. He's putting books neatly (!) back on the shelf. Oh, here he comes! He goes over to the shelf and helps himself to the bucket of Legos, which he carries back to the book corner.

9:10 Sarah approaches his corner; I don't see what she's doing, but Thomas yells "Stop!" I say to Sarah, "I think he wants to play with that by himself." Sarah takes some beads over to a table, leaving Thomas alone.

9:15 Jimmy runs over to Thomas in the book corner. I am trying to watch them over the shelf without intruding. Jimmy reaches into the bucket of Legos, and Thomas does not object. Now both are sitting side-by-side on a pillow, fitting Lego pieces together, and talking. They're nice and cozy.

9:20 Uh oh, they've made guns. "Freeze up, everybody," says Jimmy, moving out into the room. "Freeze up, everybody," says Thomas, following. "We have guns," says Thomas to a nearby teacher. "No," she says, "we don't have guns at school." (But they already do! Do I talk like that too?) "Can you make a rocket ship to take off from Cape Kennedy for the moon, or maybe a magic wand, instead?" I wonder what will happen. It's hard, but I'm going to stick to my observer role and not say anything right now . . . will wait and see.

9:30 They're both back in the corner with the Legos. "I have a gun," Jimmy says to no one in particular. He retrieves an alphabet puzzle from our (now tidy) table and takes it to work on back in the book corner. Quiet conversation between Thomas and Jimmy, with Thomas piecing together Legos next to Jimmy doing puzzle.

9:35 T. and J. have wandered out of the book corner. Jimmy is watching another child painting at the easel. Holding his Lego construction, Thomas wanders into the blocks. To me: "I made this gun myself." I say, "Thomas, a gun is not okay here. But may I show you how to give it some wings?" He does not run away! He hands the Lego gun to me, and I add 5 or 6 pieces on both sides so it now has an airplane shape. I offer the airplane/rocket ship to him. He holds it, examining the construction. He walks away, talking to himself. Jimmy runs over to him: "Gimme that gun!" Thomas defends it, yelling "You can't have it! It's a rocket ship, look!" Jimmy backs off. He retreats to the corner and starts digging through the bucket of Legos for some pieces too.

9:40 Jimmy has been intent on Legos for several minutes now. Thomas looks around for him and when he sees J. with the Legos, T. joins him. Now they are side by side again, both piecing together Lego structures, intently. Wow! Look at that! Jimmy hands T. a piece from his own pile. More intent building by both.

9:45 Jimmy comes away from Legos with a complicated gun. He is roaming and shooting, but taking care not to point the gun at anybody. Two girls have joined him, making shooting noises. Part of his gun falls off. "See, you stupid!" he yells as he gets down on the floor to fix it. "Me?" asks one of the girls? "No, the other girl," says Jimmy.

9:50 A teacher is moving around the room, telling children it's time to clean up for outside play. Some children are really helping with clean up. I approach Thomas, still working with Legos, and ask, "Thomas, can we store your rocket ship up here, on the counter, and before lunch I will make a drawing of it for you? I need you to help with clean up too."

9:55 A teacher says: "Ok, please use the toilets and wash your hands so we can go outside." Most children do. Thomas is reluctant to put up his rocket ship. I am waiting. He is fiddling with several more Legos, buying time. He starts to put it away, takes it out to fix it again, then puts it carefully on the shelf and starts toward the bathroom. I tell him "thank you." He meets Jimmy, who has been disarmed and has put on his jacket.

10:00 Jimmy greets Thomas, "Hurry up buddy! Let's go run!"

Thomas heads straight for the cubbies. I say "Use the bathroom before getting dressed, please." He does!

Written later: After outside play, when I said, "Thomas, do you want me to draw your rocket ship?" his reply was, "No! I want more Legos, now!" But it was time for circle, and I had to say "No building right now, it's circle time." He began to fuss and whimper, reaching up to the shelf for the structure. I made a hasty decision to avoid a power struggle, saying "Thomas, let's compromise. You can't build, but you can hold the Lego rocket ship while you sit at circle." He quieted down, nodded, and I handed it to him. Amazing! He sat at circle and even joined in when everyone chanted Five Little Monkeys.

What I learned: Thomas played for an HOUR and Jimmy for 40 minutes, mostly in serious construction with Legos. They were able to be friends and do dramatic play. Thomas changed his idea when redirected. Jimmy didn't, but he was careful not to shoot people. I'm glad he was given some leeway; he's a little boy trying to adjust to a new place and people. Neither finds preschool a comfortable place to be yet, but I think they both had a pretty good morning. I was so pleased when Thomas responded to my redirection and request to put the Lego structure up temporarily, AND when Jimmy came to find him before heading outside. I have a better idea of who each of them is, and I think I like them better than before.

Focused observation enabled this teacher to understand, much better than she had, two children whose behavior she usually found troublesome. She discovered some real strengths in their absorbed playing and parallel construction play, which included cooperation and conversation as well. They were enjoying being together and having private space to work in. These were 3-year-olds who received a lot of necessary power *on*; here they were inventing ways to be powerful. Watching them, the teacher got interested in their play. She moved past her pressing management question–What can I do about this child?–to child-centered questions: What interests him? What issues is he dealing with? What does he know? What might he learn next?

BUILDING ON A CHILD'S STRENGTHS

A teacher who understands children better is, indeed, likely to like them better. And she can communicate her feelings to parents, some of whom are also puzzled and frustrated by their children. At Jefferson preschool Kelly's mother has told his teacher that she is running out of patience with his behavior toward his little brother and toward the children next door. Kelly wants very much to make friends, the teacher has observed, but other children often reject him. In his disappointment he looks for someone or something to knock around.

Kelly's teacher also finds Kelly challenging. She has had to make a conscious effort to observe his behavior at its best, looking for strengths that might serve him in building the relationships he craves. His active interest in written words is something she is able to appreciate and capitalize on, in her own relationship with him and in planning activities to challenge him and the other 4s.

The activity described below was stimulated in part by her observations of Kelly's, Luis's, and Barbara's interest in writing. As she participated in it, she was able to gather more observational data on their development of competence.

On a previous day the children made drawings with chalk on purple construction paper. These have been laminated as book covers, with sheets of newsprint paper stapled between. The teacher hands them out to the children, one by one, as they sit on the rug together.

TEACHER: Kelly, here's yours.
KELLY: Thanks!
TEACHER: You're welcome.
KELLY: Does it have papers in it?
TEACHER: What could you do with it if it has papers in it?
KELLY: You could write in it. (*He explores it, pleased.*)
TEACHER: Now we're moving to the tables and we're going to make pictures in the books and maybe *we* can write in them. OK?

The table is set up with baskets of crayons, and pencils and pens. The teacher sits with the children, available to write words if asked.

KELLY: I made a hurricane.

TEACHER (*writing*): Kelly made a hurricane. (*Kelly reads it.*)

LUIS: Can you make a car?

TEACHER: I'll write car for you. Where do you want me to write car?

SUSANA: Teacher! I wrote my name.

BARBARA (*drawing on every page with crayon and scribble-writing on every page with pen*): I write my name too.

LUIS: I'm making numbers! Teacher, look at my numbers.

KELLY: There's my race track.

TEACHER: Want me to write?

KELLY: Kelly made this race track. How do you write race track?

TEACHER: I'll show you.

KELLY: I want a longer one. (*He enlarges the period she has made.*) This is another race track.

Luis is now making numbers for Kelly.

KELLY: Zoo. Kelly made a zoo. This is a race track in a zoo. (*He scribbles. Then he carefully writes an O—"and a Z," he says.*) This is a race track in a zoo.

LUIS: This is a race track in a zoo.

KELLY (*coloring with a whole handful of crayons*): Luis! Look, Luis! Luis: Teacher, lookit. I made a door. And a house. And a car. . . . And a motorcycle in the house. It went brr brrm . . . I'm not finished.

Drawing, scribbling, writing, and oral language absorb all the children for 20 minutes. Toward the end, Kelly tries disappearing under the table, where Barbara and Luis join him. The teacher asks them to come out and put away their new books for now. Kelly reappears: "I'm back. I'm not invisible anymore."

(Sandra Rangel, observer)

WHO IS THIS CHILD?

Observation during self-directed play permits attention to the uniqueness of each child. Play and language, like image-making and writing, reflect what matters most to the child. To master writing, as a 6- to 8-year-old (and beyond), it is necessary to find one's voice (Ashton-Warner, 1963; Dyson, 1989; Graves, 1983; Johnson, 1987). To master play, as a 3- to 5-year-old, it is equally necessary to find one's voice, an aspect of development of self-concept. The young child who is a master player has a sense of agency, using play to represent herself and her ideas, as she will do through her drawing and, later, her writing.

In *The Ambiguity of Play,* play scholar Brian Sutton-Smith suggests that play is a form of adaptation used by different people in various ways and resulting in the survival of the species: "There are considerable differences between physically skillful players and those who are intellectually skillful. . . . It would seem likely, therefore, that such individual play skills would be differentiated just as other human abilities are. . . . The survival of the species may have been due to the distinctive contributions of individuals" (1997, pp. 46–47).

To help all children master play, teachers might well try Graves's (1983) advice for getting to know each child. In three columns:

1. Try listing from memory all the children in your class. (Then draw a line, and add below it those you have forgotten.)
2. For each child, list his or her experiences and interests.
3. For each interest, indicate whether and how you have specifically confirmed it for the child. How have you helped him/her to play it, talk about it, recognize it as valuable?

As Graves (1983) explains:

> The ultimate object of the column exercise is to be able to fill in all three columns, to carry the *unique territories of information about the children in memory.* Those children for whom it is most difficult to come up with a territory of information are *those who need it most.* They are often the children who find it difficult to choose topics, to locate a territory of their own. They perceive themselves as nonknowers, persons without turf, with no place to stand. (pp. 22–23)

To locate a territory of their own, children need plenty of time to explore and choose. At Second Street child care center, the staff has been experimenting with extending the outdoor playtime by having only half the 4-year-olds at a time go in for teacher-planned small-group activities. Indoors there's "'less mess, less noise," a teacher assistant says, pleased. Outdoors children who have had plenty of time for physical activity start gravitating toward easels and table activities, where they spontaneously create shapes and colors, letters and numbers. There are long turns–two or three turns or even six–for painting, and if more room is needed, paper and paints can be put on the table, too. The teacher is relaxed with only half the group to supervise.

LARRY (*repeating shapes that look like D's*): I'm painting 4's.
TEACHER: And you're 4. A lot of children here are 4. (*When he's through, she*

admires the colors in his painting.) That yellow matches my sweater, doesn't it? And you made some green that is the same as your socks!

VANESSA (*arriving*): I'm going to make two pictures, OK?

The teacher prints "Vanessa" on the paper. Vanessa takes the marker and copies her name, easily. Instead of painting, she continues to use the marker to form letters, make named scribbles, and finally fill up the page with swirls. Watching Vanessa, studies of emergent writing make sense: young children combine drawing and writing to express themselves. They do not distinguish between the two mediums (Sulzby, 1986).

LARRY (*very interested*): Why's she writing her name? She gonna write it again?

TEACHER: She's practicing her name.

LARRY: Can I practice my name too?

TEACHER: Yes, when she's done.

LARRY: You gonna help me? (*He goes off on a bike.*)

TEACHER (*naming letters with a highly motivated Vanessa*): You have made a lot of letters that I can read!

Edward, who has been painting on the other side of the easel for a long long time, is done, and the teacher invites Larry for his turn. She prints his name. He takes the marker and experiments with making controlled scribbles. Inspired by Vanessa, he draws a few letter-like forms, but then he discovers dots, counting as he makes a great many of them. Then he begins making scribbles and naming them.

LARRY: This is my mommy. . . . No, that isn't my mommy. This is a spider.

TEACHER: Where's your mommy?

LARRY: I'm gonna make her. Here. . . . This is my bed. . . . This is my brother. . . . Mama.

From this play with drawing and writing tools, the teacher recognizes that Larry and Vanessa have different skills (see Figure 7.1). Among the eight children who by now are all drawing and painting, she is aware of the wide range of ability and focus. Each is discovering patterns and practicing and elaborating them. Vanessa, she notices, is now joyously painting her hand with magenta "blood" and then covering both hands with yellow, making "gloves." With her painty hands she makes prints all over a sheet of paper on the table.

Stephanie doesn't like paint on her hands, but she likes Vanessa's good idea. She traces her hand with a marker. Vanessa likes that idea, and soon almost everyone is using markers to make hands, tracing their own or drawing freehand. Richard tells the teacher that his is a baseball glove. Edward's hands have four fingers and a wrist. Vanessa's hands have five fingers; she has done a whole page of them, with different colored markers. Now she closes each with a line and adds feet to some! (See Figure 7.2.)

FIGURE 7.1. "I can practice my name."

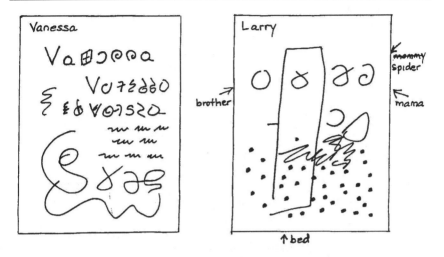

COMMUNICATING TO PARENTS AND OTHER ADULTS

For an hour, these 4-year-olds explored symbol-making, being self-directed in their use of paints and markers outdoors and in the design of collages indoors. As they worked, they talked. Because collage construction needs no explanation—materials attractively organized on a table are themselves an invitation to explore—the teacher was free to record the children's words, in English and Spanish. Thanks to his initiative, the walls of the classroom and foyer are covered with children's artwork, photos of some of their activities, and their words. Together with family members, and with each other when they have an errand to the kitchen or visit another classroom, children look for their work with their names in the displays and talk about what they've done. Teachers' narratives of children's play and words label children's

FIGURE 7.2. Hands

representations, making the process of children's learning visible to parents and other visitors. Because the displays of children's work stimulate parents' interest, they are a provocation to participate, along with teachers and children, in this learning community. Displays communicate: Important things happen here. Children are learning through their activities and play. We invite you to reflect on what children may be learning, to ask questions, and to discuss your ideas with your child and with us (Curtis & Carter, 2008; Rinaldi, 2006).

"All they do here is play," worries a parent concerned about her child's future success in school. Teachers who are able to take parents' perspective can recognize critical comments as opportunities for conversation on the ways children learn through play. Some teachers provide further information by posting descriptions of what children may learn in each of the free-choice centers. See Figure 7.3 for an example from Anne Solomon, a kindergarten teacher in California's Rocklin district.

Communication books are another way in which teachers and parents share their observations of the child's activities and learning. At the Ottawa Inuit Children's Centre, where children come to the program by van and parents do not visit regularly, it's routine for every child to carry his book home in his backpack. Teacher Natasha likes to write a short story about an event in the child's school day for the family's evening pleasure. On their return, communication books often contain a parent's comments or a story in exchange.

FIGURE 7.3. What Children Learn in Block Play

BLOCKS

- ROLE PLAYING: building a farm, a city, a school, a house and acting out the parts
- PROBLEM SOLVING: figuring out how to do something and experimenting w/ the materials
- COOPERATIVE PLAY: working w/ friends to make things together
- ORAL LANGUAGE: talking about what's being made and how it's made
- PATTERN: using blocks to build a fence, road or similar buildings
- REPRESENTATION: building something to look like something the child knows about
- PART TO WHOLE: seeing that individual blocks can be used to build something even larger
- MATCHING: making 2 roads of equal length - making 2 towers exactly alike
- CREATIVITY: creating one's own ideas
- SELF-ESTEEM: feeling good about what is created - pride in one's accomplishments
- MEASUREMENT: figuring out how many blocks are needed to make equal sides of buildings
- CLASSIFYING: in cleaning up children sort blocks according to similarities
- BALANCE: experimenting w/ blocks to make things that don't have 1 side that falls over
- EXTENSION OF LITERATURE: creating something from a story that's been heard
- SHAPE & SIZE VOCABULARY: rectangle, square, triangle, long, short, etc.
- SIZE RELATIONSHIP: longer, shorter, long, longer, longest

Natasha sometimes sits on the floor to be available to children during free play while she writes in their communication books. One day, while we visited, she described for William's grandparents his dramatic play with miniature marine animals. That day William used multiple voices as he animated various miniatures in an ocean habitat (the water table). In Rachel's book Natasha told her mom about making bannock (a type of bread made by First Nations people) in literacy circle.

In preschools and kindergartens teachers communicate their assessments of children's learning and development to parents in conferences, interviews, and written reports. At Live Oak preschool teachers and practicum students write twice-yearly narrative reports describing children's physical, social-emotional, language, and cognitive development. As part of their college coursework, students work with teachers to develop portfolios for each family. Using a range of observation tools—running records, anecdotes, narratives, photos, checklists, and samples of children's work—they analyze progress using an evidence-based continuum of development.

The kindergartens at Second Street School used to have report cards on which teachers were required to rate each child's progress as satisfactory/unsatisfactory. With support from the principal, teachers engaged in a year-long cooperative effort to create a profile that mapped the progress of a child's learning, with no developmental level labeled unsatisfactory. Parents were pleased, and teachers found the profiles useful in focusing their observations of children (Jones & Meade-Roberts, 1991; Meade-Roberts, 1988). Within its broad categories—literacy skills, numeracy skills, curiosity and creativity, physical development, social skills, and ability to meet school and teacher expectations—a teacher watched for children's progress toward his overarching goals for their development: competence in (1) representation and (2) relationship. Under *representation,* he looked closely at language, dramatic play, construction and creation with materials, and developing literacy and numeracy. Under *relationship,* he was alert to children's caring for others as shown in communication, cooperation, empathy, and conflict resolution. Teachers and parents knew that children who were responsible, thoughtful group members and confident, creative representers would be ready for whatever schooling came next.

Schools that are places of collaborative teacher research—How could we do this better? What will we learn if we create a new assessment tool?—often discover newly effective practices for teaching children and communicating with families. The kindergarten teachers at Second Street School invented an assessment system that respected each child's individuality, a grassroots effort that reflected a valuing of children's and families' rights. Looking back, their design to assess children's abilities using an evidence-based developmental trajectory foreshadowed national education policies and states' adoption of learning standards, currently used to predict, assess, and plan for learning.

In classrooms where children all do identical projects, different learnings take place and different messages are communicated to parents. The walls reflect adult rather than child activity: "We are learning about bunnies [or fall, or St. Patrick's Day], and our teacher has cleverly cut out shapes for us to glue ears on [or has made a collection of pictures], to remind us of the theme she has chosen for us."

An observer at Second Street School, visiting when the classroom has a rabbit in residence, is admiring posted representations by teacher and children. Above the cage is a list of the children's invented "Rules for Peter/Reglos para el conejo: Don't drop Peter the rabbit. Don't hide him. Don't put things inside the cage. Don't squeeze the water. . . ." Next to the rules is Stephanie's spontaneous painting of a large rabbit, with a small cage in the corner of the page.

The substitute teacher complains to the observer, "These children get away with too much. I think they need to learn right and wrong. I'm used to teaching numbers and colors, but here they won't let us use templates. Not even bunnies."

"But look at Stephanie's rabbit," says the observer. "Isn't that a more rabbity rabbit than any model made by a teacher?"

"Well, maybe," says the substitute teacher. "But that Stephanie, she's smart. Most of the children can't do that, you know."

Because Stephanie's teacher respects each child's abilities to create her own representations, the substitute teacher will remain frustrated. But she is not alone; many adults who work with children find joy in cutting out patterns and shopping for commercial holiday decorations. That's what their teachers did when they were children in school; now it's their turn to play teacher. Walls decorated with such things reassure other adults, including parents, that there's really curriculum here. Thoughtful communication is necessary to help adults understand children's need to make their own representations and see their own words in writing.

COMMUNICATING TO CHILDREN

In classrooms where children's work all looks alike, the children are practicing the teacher's ideas. When we encourage children to create for themselves, they learn that there are many ways of doing things. Take kites, for example. Sometimes teachers, who know what kites look like, cut out diamond shapes for all the children to glue tails on. But real kites do come in different shapes, and pretend kites can come in even more.

At Madison West preschool, Georgina Villarino decided to encourage divergent thinking by putting out all sorts of materials—paper in various shapes, paper plates, circles with holes, hearts, feathers, flowers, tissue-paper strips, yarn—and tools—scissors, tape, glue, a hole punch, and a stapler—in the art area. The splendidly divergent results, with children's words added, now fly on a large bulletin board, light blue above and green below (see Figure 7.4).

"Children really pay attention to a bulletin board like this," says Georgina. "They made it themselves, and it's easy to tell whose work is whose. They look for their names. They move chairs over to the bulletin board and stand on them and look at their words and touch their kites and talk about them. And they show their parents. The parents are beginning to understand that children are learning here, even though the teaching may look different to them."

In the role of scribe, writing children's words for them to see, teachers take brief notes every day. In contrast, the notes Thomas and Jimmy's teacher was making at the beginning of this chapter prompted an awed visitor to ask, "Do you write this much very often?"

"Of course not," said the teacher. "I like to write, and so note-taking is fun for me. I wish I had that much time to observe every day, but I rarely take that much time to observe! This was desperation time. I really needed to know what was going on with those kids."

"So those notes were for you," observed the visitor. "You were making a child study for yourself."

"Yes, and to share in a team meeting, so we can make a plan for both boys," explained the teacher. "But the quality of play I saw when I was paying attention convinced me that it's our expectations that need to be changed. It's only when we interrupt them that those boys get outrageous. They're very young, and they're not yet tuned in to our routines. Jimmy was eager

FIGURE 7.4. "How can we make a kite?"

to help, once he'd had time enough for the transition and realized what was going on. Observing helps us recognize what's going on for them.

"I even showed some of what I'd written to Thomas's mother, to let her know I was pleased with his long attention span. She was a bit concerned about the gun play, and that gave us a chance to talk about what he watches on TV. So it wasn't just for me, after all."

This teacher, like others we've described, makes regular notes of children's language and posts them, along with children's paintings and drawings, on the wall. It's the parents and older 4-year-olds who are most interested, she finds; the 3-year-olds are still absorbed in exploring materials and constructing their own symbols, including Lego guns. She finds that extra effort is required to represent the whole range of children's work, including dramatization, language, and constructions made of blocks or Legos or other materials that get put away rather than taken home (Kuschner, 1989).

Constructions can be saved and labeled for short periods of time; children can write their own "PLS sv" signs or dictate their words to adults. Since this preschool has both morning and afternoon groups, children often choose something to save for the other group to see. Suitably labeled–"Luz and Ben built this airport"–it awaits discovery by the other children, who are helped to read the sign, talk about it if they wish, and then add to it or dismantle it as they pursue their own ideas with the blocks (Olivia Rivera, personal communication, 1990). When children share a classroom with other children they never see, messages are important!

Communicating with children is a two-way process. Vanessa and Larry and their friends let their teacher know, by their action, what they know about writing and painting–and hands. The teacher followed up this activity by choosing to serve as the "memory" of the group (New, 1990, p, 8); on the day that followed, she reminded the children of what they had done and added her representations to theirs. Finding their "hands" irresistible, she decided to sustain this interest, moving into the role of teacher as planner of emergent curriculum (see Chapter 8).

ACCOUNTABILITY: HOW DO WE KNOW THEY'RE LEARNING?

In many settings, neither teachers nor children have permission to play at school. Learning is serious; "let's get down to business." Parents and administrators, and many teachers, are skeptical if children are "only playing." Their common sense and the behaviorist theory that guides American education generate a view of teaching as engineering: "a structured process of shaping behavior according to predetermined specifications much as industrial work involved the shaping of raw materials into prespecified products"

(Donmoyer, 1981, p. 14). Consistent with this imagery, behavior modification approaches to teaching use the metaphor of the marketplace, a system based on payment rather than on giving. These methods "inevitably promote a dichotomy between work and play, or—more broadly—between doing something because one has to, and doing something because one wants to" (Franklin & Biber, 1977, p. 8).

In a society focused on technology and consumption, the popularity of this view is understandable. But popular wisdom and developmental theory are at odds. In reviewing the relative places of behaviorism and Piaget's constructivism in the history of psychology, Kamii (1985) explains:

> All sciences begin by studying surface, observable, and limited phenomena, and by explaining them with mere common sense. It is not surprising that psychologists, too, began by studying behavior, which is observable and easier to study than complicated phenomena such as human knowledge and morality. Teaching by telling and rewards makes good common sense, but the time has come for educators to go beyond mere common sense. (p. 7)

In constructivist theory, Kamii explains, children learn by going through one level after another of being "wrong." Science, and education, develop in the same way. A developmental approach in early childhood education represents a more complex and inclusive theory of learning than does the engineering metaphor. It uses a growth metaphor, in which the teacher is not an efficient engineer but a nurturer of play—of the child's spontaneous action. This definition is nowhere found in familiar conceptions of teaching.

The teacher who would nurture play, then, has both a political and a moral obligation to be accountable to those unfamiliar with the rationale for this view of learning. While skepticism about the value of play is widespread, it is no accident that parents in those groups that have traditionally lacked power in our economic system are particularly concerned when teachers let children play. Their children have been ill-served in our schools, often by teachers who lacked belief in their ability to learn. "You teach my kid!" is an understandable and justifiable expectation of any parent, and especially by those whose suspicion that their children are victims of institutional racism or classism is well founded (Clemens, 1983; Delpit, 1988).

Our emphasis on the teacher's roles of scribe, assessor, communicator, and planner is a response to these genuine concerns. We have found that educators who share parents' concern about teaching children move with pleasure into the role of scribe, which clearly supports the development of literacy and keeps teachers responsibly active during children's play. Scribed products serve as effective communication to parents and other adults. Attention to the development of literacy scripts, by making writing materials and books generously available and responding to children's play with them, further supports children's growth in the skills that matter most in schools.

The critical and divergent thinking that children practice in play and problem-solving contribute significantly to self-regulation and the higher-order thinking skills they will later need in school, though these outcomes may be more difficult to convince parents of, especially parents who value obedience and rote performance. Shirley Brice Heath (1983) describes the children of Roadville, a White working-class community, whose parents expect young children at home to listen to stories read from books, answer questions following the reading, and do workbook tasks. "Adults in Roadville believe that instilling in children the proper use of words and understanding the meaning of the written word are important for both their educational and religious success" (p. 60). However, books and stories are separate from the rest of life in Roadville, and families do not play with words or ideas.

Roadville children do well in the early years of school. They have learned the surface rules of the school game: Pay attention, do what you're told, and respect the written word. They are stumped, however, when asked to create or critique stories or respond to hypothetical questions.

> Thus their initial successes in reading, being good students, following orders, and adhering to school norms of participating in lessons begin to fall away rapidly about the time they enter the fourth grade. As the importance and frequency of questions and reading habits with which they are familiar declines in the higher grades, they have no way of keeping up or of seeking help in learning what it is they do not even know they don't know. (p. 84)

Creating and critiquing stories and dealing with "what if?" questions are skills learned through play and playful dialogue. The play of 3- to 5-year-olds is a crucial developmental stage in children's continuing construction of knowledge and in their learning to learn. To be accountable for children's learning while nurturing their play, teachers need to respond thoughtfully and imaginatively to the expectations of others, while retaining their responsibility as curriculum decision-makers.

CHAPTER 8

Teacher
as Planner

"Did you see what I put on the wall?" the teacher at Second Street child care center asks Richard and Edward. "My hands!" says Edward promptly, recognizing both his name and his drawings. Richard's "baseball glove" is there, too, but Richard ignores it; he has spotted the real baseball glove the teacher has put on the shelf below, together with several pairs of gloves in different sizes. He tries it on. Edward puts on gloves with rabbit-fur cuffs and strokes his cheek with them. Larry arrives. "Who did them?" he asks, pointing to a row of cut-out paper hands along the bottom of the bulletin board.

"I did," says the teacher. "I traced my hand, and I cut it out."

"Can I cut too?" asks Larry.

"Sure," says the teacher, pleased with his interest. Paper, pencils, and scissors are already on the table. Larry and Richard go off to practice cutting, which is challenge enough for them; hands are temporarily forgotten.

The teacher has lots of ideas for continuing with hands, though. A light projected against a sheet will offer an opportunity for shadow play; shadows can be made outdoors, too. She remembers fondly the animal shapes her grandpa used to make with hand shadows on her bedroom wall. She also remembers the Mummenschanz mime troupe she once saw, with white- and colored-gloved hands moving against a black background. Silently, the gloved hands masquerade as fantastic characters expressing human behaviors and emotions—entertaining and provocative to an imaginative 4-year-old. She is inspired by that memory to try lining the puppet stage with black paper and finding more gloves. She wonders what happened to that silky elbow-length red pair they had with the dress-up clothes. On a rainy day, perhaps the children will enjoy seeing one of the short videos of mime theater on the internet (www.Mummenschanz.com).

The assistant teacher knows American Sign Language (ASL), and he has been teaching signs to the whole group, all of whom are hearing children (Brereton, 2010). Most of the children enjoy using the sign language vocabulary they know when they say *mommy, daddy, grandpa,* and *grandma*; for foods—*pizza, milk,* and *apple*; for requests—*please, stop, thank you,* and *help*; and for some feelings—*angry, happy, sad, love,* and *sorry* (www.lifeprint.com). It is encouraging that Lichung and Wong, newcomer Mandarin-speaking brothers, are comfortable using signs when interacting with other children and the adults. The boys seem to understand some English, but neither of them is speaking it yet.

Outdoors, Vanessa is spontaneously painting her hands; that's another way to make gloves. Experimenting with clay one morning, Graham was "washing" his hands and arms up to his elbows with slip, holding them out to admire their interesting brown tone. Hands come in different sizes—and skin colors, too, without benefit of paint or clay; what about photographing everyone's hands and playing matching games with the pictures and the real hands? As adults and children talk, and create, and compare, and question, they'll keep on learning together.

If the children are interested, their ideas and the teachers' will be integrated into a long-term project derived from children's spontaneous play and image-making. Such projects challenge children's thinking and extend their play (Helm & Katz, 2010; Katz & Chard, 2000; Stacey, 2009; Wien, 2008). Perhaps some parents will get involved, and the outcomes are likely to be stimulating to everyone. But planning for play doesn't begin with projects, in which teachers set the direction and sometimes, in their enthusiasm, take over. Planning is an emergent process in which play has priority. The outcome is an emergent curriculum—one in which both adults and children exercise initiative and make decisions.

EMERGENT CURRICULUM

> The term *emergent curriculum* thus captures a seeming paradox: an intentional course is implied by the use of the word *curriculum*, derived from the Latin *currere*, meaning to run a course or make one's way around a known route. But paradoxically, the course of this curriculum is not known at the outset. It is emergent—that is, its trajectory develops as a consequence of the logic of the problem, the particular connections that develop as participants bring their own genuine responses to the topic and collaboratively create the course to follow out of these multiple connections. (Wien, 2008, pp. 5–6)

Any curriculum is the outcome of someone's choices among all the things in the world that there are for children to learn. In an emergent curriculum, the choices are made by the children and by the adults who know them.

However, an emergent curriculum is never built only on children's interests. Teachers are people with interests of their own that are worth sharing with children. By doing some things teachers themselves like, they model knowledge and enthusiasms–even adults keep on learning–and stay interested in teaching (Jones & Nimmo, 1994).

Values held for children's learning in the school and community, the family and culture, help to determine curriculum content. Curriculum also emerges from the things, people, and events in the environment, and from all the issues that arise in the course of living together day to day. Caregiving, expression of feelings, and resolving problems and interpersonal conflicts are not interruptions to the curriculum; they are basic curriculum.

"Lesson plans," written before the fact, are often required of teachers by directors who wish to ensure that careful thought is given to the activities provided for children. Any thoughtful curriculum is planned both to be responsive to where children are and to take them somewhere, in the direction of agreed-upon goals that are aligned with state child outcome standards (Bodrova, Leong, & Shore, 2004; NAEYC, 2009). If a curriculum is pre-planned toward specific objectives or skills without considering the unique ways children develop and learn, it is typically linear, with only one way to go. But learning, as it happens, is nonlinear, diverging along unexpected paths as new connections are made. Teachers may forget that children matter more than their good planning. Curriculum is for children. Paying careful attention, a teacher knows to spontaneously deter from her original plan if it does not support a child's engagement and competence (Gonzalez-Mena & Stonehouse, 2008).

For this reason a web is a more effective planning tool than an outline or chart. Teachers find that webs are useful when brainstorming curriculum possibilities, and if a chart is a program regularity, a web will complement the charting process. It's easy to include information on curriculum webs for parents about the developmental and learning outcomes for children participating in experiences on a topic (Helm, 2008). A web leaves plenty of space for add-ons at the inspiration of everyone involved. (An example of webbing is presented under "Introducing a New Topic" later in this chapter.)

Emergent curriculum planning relies heavily on observation, and it is best represented after the fact. The outcomes are broad rather than narrowly specified. The teacher makes no claim that he will teach 80% of the children to name eight colors by December 1–the sort of behavioral objective that builds in plenty of room for failure by both teacher and children (Jones, 1983). Instead, he provides a choice-full environment where children, as they explore and play, will have many opportunities to, for example:

- Hear and use oral language
- Explore varied art media
- See and discuss written words
- Practice solving interpersonal problems
- Investigate and ask questions about the natural environment
- Explore and order materials using pattern, shapes, and counting
- Acquire various physical skills
- Notice the colors of different objects, and hear and use color names during conversations about these objects

The teacher's preplanning thus includes the contents and organization of the physical environment and the time schedule, and the stories, songs, activities, and conversations to be included in each day, which are selected for about a week at a time, with room for last-minute changes. Any themes to be emphasized may be indicated for several months or for a whole year, with the expectation that some unpredicted interests will emerge along the way. There is, however, an absence of "The children will learn____" objectives. Instead, the children will have opportunities to do____, and the teacher will learn by observing them and thus continue to plan thoughtfully for children's construction of knowledge based on their doing.

By providing materials and interactions in organized space and time, teachers enable the play to get started. They continue to pay attention to what children are actually doing and learning, modifying plans on the spot when necessary and responding to children's ideas and interests with spur-of-the-moment teaching. Exploration and physical action come first, and then mastery of play. It is when children are well established as competent players and group members that they are ready for challenges like the project on *hands* described above or the investigation of *snails* described below. In any group, some children thrive on the sustained involvement a project investigation offers, and others are less interested in deeper inquiry on one topic.

Three- , four- , and five-year-olds are "wigglers and doers," and pre-school and kindergarten teachers " . . . are rigorously academic because they keep goals in mind as they interact with children in their play and exploration" (Gronlund, 2006, p. 144). When teachers plan and make observations, they identify child outcome standards. In the next story about a dinosaur bone dig, the children are helped to " . . . develop curiosity, initiative, self-direction, and persistence" (p. 94), a social/emotional outcome in many states' lists of standards.

Teachers discover children's skills and interests during observations of play. In the role of planner, a teacher may focus on the environment as it supports play or on the playscripts themselves.

LOOKING AT THE ENVIRONMENT

How is a selected area of the room or yard being used by children? Over a period of days or weeks, does anyone look at books or choose puzzles or build with blocks? If not, should that activity be put away for a while? Or, if the teacher thinks an activity is important, can she think of a way to reorganize it or move it or add other materials to it, to provide the attraction of novelty and to increase clarity and complexity? Could she develop a curriculum theme that might stimulate children's interest in those materials?

Out of observation comes action. The teacher in the following episode began with a management problem, observed carefully in order to understand a child's needs, and came up with an idea for play that she knew she would enjoy and predicted the children would, too. She's an experienced teacher, and her predictions are often sound.

At Second Street School, sand play among the younger children has recently been characterized by throwing rather than purposeful digging or building. Abdou, a particularly high-energy 3-year-old, repeatedly tries the adults' patience; they have been tempted to forbid him access to the sand in his more excitable moments. But there's so much sand, and so much to be learned by playing in it, that instead the teacher has invented a new playscript that she hopes will make digging more interesting.

On a day when both the assistant teacher and an experienced parent volunteer are available for indoor play, the teacher invites a small group of children to come outside with her. "Let's sit at the table so you can see my book," she says. It's a story about a missing dinosaur bone. She shows them the pictures for a few minutes, then asks if they'd like to look for the missing bone. "I think we should try the sand," she says, handing out spoons for digging. There are tools in the sand, too, and Abdou replaces his spoon with a large scoop, with which he digs vigorously. And there are "bones" to be found in the sand—Lincoln log bones, which the teacher had buried earlier in the day.

BEN: We're using our muscles.
ABDOU (*showing the teacher the muscle in his arm*): Big muscles.
TEACHER: Good—the better to dig bones with!
Abdou tosses sand and gets it in his hair. He complains.
TEACHER: Abdou, you have to be careful. When you're archeologists you have to dig carefully.
Sarah gets in Abdou's way. He hits her with his scoop.
TEACHER: Abdou, you can't hit your friends.

Clearly, they are friends. They're talking together eagerly. Abdou shows Sarah his muscle. He digs vigorously.

TEACHER: Think you've just about found all the bones?
ABDOU: No, not yet. Digging, digging. I found a bone! (*All the children are digging. Abdou tosses sand out of the box.*)
TEACHER: Remember, Abdou, not so high.

He makes a concerted effort to toss the sand lower. He is enjoying the large-muscle action that the rhythm of dig-and-toss provides. He experiments with a smooth swinging movement that sends the sand out in a lovely arc.

ABDOU (*digging hard again*): I found another bone!
SARAH: I found a little bone. I'm the bone collector.
BEN (*to Sarah, who is tossing sand*): Are you making a hole, Sarah?
ABDOU: Stop! Don't get sand on me.
SARAH: Gimme my spoon.
ABDOU: That's not your spoon, that's my spoon.
SARAH (*grabbing*): That's mine!
ABDOU: No, I want it back! (*He is now crying loudly.*)
TEACHER: Find any more bones lately?
ABDOU (*stopping his crying as abruptly as he started*): No.
SARAH: Teacher, I feel a bone in here.
TEACHER: You feel a bone? (*Teacher begins digging, and Abdou helps her.*)
SARAH: Yeah, Abdou, we find all the bones, right? It's a baby bone.
TEACHER: We have to dig carefully. There's a baby one in the sandbox.
SARAH (*talking to Ben and Abdou about their bone collection*): We gonna glue them.
TEACHER: When you glue them, what will you have?
SARAH: A skeleton! Dinosaur skeleton! Like at the museum with Daddy.
TEACHER: Oh, you start with bones, you get a dinosaur skeleton?
SARAH: Yeah.

"The children do know they're Lincoln logs, not dinosaur bones, don't they?" said the assistant teacher, who had come outside in time to overhear this thought. "Yes, they know. But they had fun pretending to look for dinosaur bones. And so did I," said the teacher. "The children may not really care about archeology, but it makes the activity more fun for me. And when I'm having fun, I have more patience with kids who throw sand. I've also been noticing that Abdou doesn't do it to bother people. He's using those big muscles—and I saw him really watching the movement of sand through the air. I think Abdou is working on self-regulation skills—helped by satisfying play with Sarah, who shares his interest in digging for dinosaur bones."

This play was sustained for a full hour. Working in a small space, 3-year-olds encounter frequent problems of territory, which their teacher helps them solve. Problem-solving is an important part of their work at this "dig." And these diggers are passionate about their work, as young children should be.

NAMING CHILDREN'S PLAYSCRIPTS

What scripts are children playing? A teacher might decide to keep a list of those she overhears or chooses to watch in action. How varied are they? Which children play which scripts? Are they imitative or creative? Do they require toys that are replicas of media characters? Are they based on good guy/bad guy themes (Levin, 2009)? Are there any scripts she might like to try to introduce, to broaden children's repertoire?

How much detailed knowledge of their scripts do children show? What do they know about procedures in medical settings, about the sequence of cooking a meal, about the behavior of airplanes and functions of trains? How rich is their vocabulary? Observation can be used to give a teacher ideas for adding props, new language, and different roles to children's play, within the script they have established. By doing so, she can see if they are ready for more details and a "thicker" plot.

At Live Oak preschool, for several days the baby doll has been bottle-fed. Today the teacher asks, "Is your baby old enough for baby food?" Camilla thinks about it. "No, she wants her bottle." She burps the baby and puts her to bed. The teacher retreats. But 2 days later, Camilla says suddenly, "Now she's old enough." The teacher has forgotten. "Who is?" "My baby," says Camilla impatiently. "She wants baby food."

Children certainly know what they want when they want it, thinks the teacher delightedly, as she goes to the shelf where she has stored several baby food containers. "Here you are. There's peaches, and cereal, and strained peas. Can you find a spoon?" Yes, Camilla can. She puts the baby in the high chair, the teacher looks for and finds a bib, and a new scene has been added to the play.

Fernando's driving script seems to be titled "Crash!" and the teacher is beginning to be concerned about the sturdiness of the bike he is riding. As he picks himself up for the fifth time, she moves toward him. "You really crashed," she acknowledges. He grins. "This is my crash car." "Does your daddy crash his car, too?" she asks. "Yep," says Fernando. "Where were you?" asks the teacher. "In my car seat. Mom and me in the back seat," says Fernando. "That must have been scary," the teacher suggests. "Real scary. Mom cried. She looked for cuts." Fernando acknowledges. "Papa was sad. The police is his friend. Then he is happy."

"What happened to the car?" asks the teacher.

"Papa taked it to the garage," says Fernando. "They fixed it."

"Does your crash car need to go to the garage?" asks the teacher.

That's a new idea for Fernando. He gets down on the ground to inspect the bike. "Yeah," he decides. "It needs a hammer right here. See?"

Zach has been listening. "My uncle Bob fixes cars," he says.

"Does he have a hammer?" asks the teacher.

"Yes," says Zach. "A hammer, and a machine that makes air for tires, a hose, and a wrench!"

"Do you think you could fix Fernando's crash car?" the teacher suggests.

Zach seriously gets down to look at it. Fernando shows him where it crashed. Zach gets a small shovel from the sandbox to use for a wrench. They are working together on it as the teacher moves on, making a mental note to bring some real tools the next day and propose building a garage for fixing cars.

INTRODUCING A NEW TOPIC

What are children doing and saying in response to curriculum content that teachers have chosen to introduce? Was the choice of topic a good one? Does it hold children's interest? Is it generating new vocabulary and stimulating conversation? Are children adding their own ideas to our planning web?

Sue Bush, who teaches 3-year-olds at Willard Children's Center, loves gardens, but gardeners don't love snails. Children are fascinated by snails.

"So one night," explains Sue, "after it rained, I went out with a flashlight and collected snails. There were dozens and dozens of them. I brought them to school and gave half of them to Joyce, for her 4-year-olds."

The snails are in a large clear container on the science shelf, with half a dozen children clustered around. Sue is taping a large sheet of dark blue paper onto one of the work tables. All the children but Alison, who is wiping the snack table, crowd around as Sue tips the snails out of their container onto the paper. They start making snail trails and climbing on one another—and on the children who want to hold them. There are plenty of snails for all the children. As the children and snails explore each other, Sue narrates what she observes.

Some of us just want to look at the snails. They don't want to touch them.

Don't put a snail on anyone else if they don't like it. Chris likes his snail to walk on his arm.

But don't put a snail on someone who doesn't.

As she talks and watches and listens, she is writing down children's words. Already, she has pages of notes. Live creatures stimulate children's language and observational skills, and sometimes fantasy.

CHRIS: Look, Sue, he's crying.

SUE: What's the matter with him?

CHRIS: He wants to get down. Here you go, snail.

Sue has decided to write down one child's snail talk each day. Yesterday she listened to Ernie. Today, on the wall above the science table, are Ernie's words (see Figure 8.1).

FIGURE 8.1. Ernie's Words About Snails

<u>Snails - Ernie</u>

Do they bite?
They move slow.
I don't want to touch it.
I touch them.
They don't bite.
Yuck! That snail slobbered on me.
Yikes!
They won't bite.
I'm making him roll.
I pick him up and put him in my hand.
They're cold, Sue.
He's crawling on my hand.
Oh, they're fighting.

Although this is the second day with snails, they've lost none of their novelty. For a full 15 minutes all the children are absorbed in snail watching and experimenting: If I cut my apple slice real small, will he eat it? How does he move? How does he drink the water we give him? When he goes inside his shell, is he sleeping? While most of the children gradually go on to other activities, a few remain with the snails for 40 minutes. Ernie moves from the snails only as far as his teacher's note pad; he leans against her to watch her writing, then gets a pencil for himself and adds his own letter-like shapes among hers. She lets him, looking on with interest. When she finally lays down the pad to put the snails away, Ernie promptly picks it up. "See my O's?" he says to Chris.

In Joyce's room next door, the 4-year-olds, who have watched the snails laying down their silvery trails, are making "snail trails" of their own on paper, using watery tempera paint in medicine droppers. Audrey gets markers and draws a page full of snails. She talks excitedly with her teacher as they count, and Joyce writes her words: "Audrey made 17 snails." At group time, as the children keep talking about snails, Joyce shows them how to write "snail" in English and "*caracol*" in Spanish.

On their lunch break, Joyce shows Sue what Audrey has just spontaneously written on a piece of paper:

SNAIL
CARACOL
AUDREY
AUDREY

Joyce and Sue agree: "This theme is working!" Not like the goldfish, Joyce remarks; we had six, and now there's only one, and no one seems to miss them. Snails, on the other hand, are stimulating absorbed exploration, of themselves, of oral language, and of the written word. The children are excited, and so are the teachers.

An arriving visitor is enthusiastically welcomed: "You've got to see this!" The visitor shares the teachers' enthusiasm, admires all the drawing and writing, and has a chance to play with the snails, too. Tentatively, she reminds the teachers of another mode of teacher play, one that had been discussed at a recent in-service: "webbing" as a way to plan and represent curriculum themes. They remember, and they're eager to try it.

Sure enough, the next time she visits, a web is posted on the wall in Joyce's room (see Figure 8.2).

"How did you do it?" the visitor asks.

"We weren't sure how we were supposed to do it, so we just sat down together during nap time with a big piece of paper. I wrote "SNAILS" in the middle of it," says Sue.

FIGURE 8.2. Snails: A Curriculum Web

"And then we looked at each other and laughed. We didn't know what to write next," Joyce says. "So we decided to put down everything we had done to begin with and then add the things that happened along the way."

The visitor is a bit puzzled. "Can you show me?" she asks. "Okay, look," says Sue. "We got out a terrarium to put the snails in so they wouldn't crawl all over the room. The kids all came around to see, and someone asked why I was putting them in there, and someone else asked where I got them, and we ended up in a long conversation about where snails live. I mentioned that I don't like them living in my garden because they eat my plants, and Chris wanted to know what they would eat at school, and I showed them the lettuce and dandelion leaves I had put in the terrarium. We talked about the foods snails need to live—leafy vegetables, no meat. Since then I've seen children saving bits of lettuce and apples from snack and lunch to see if the snails will like it. We picked nasturtium leaves in the garden."

"I wanted a related art activity, and so I made up snail trails," Joyce explains. "The children have used droppers with paint before, and they enjoy them. This was a new name for the activity, which really stimulated several children's interest. And then Audrey went on to drawing and writing; she's just turned 5, and she's really into writing. Her mother is so pleased."

"I hadn't thought of any snail books, but they loved *One Snail and Me*" (McLeod, 1961), says Sue. "So do I. Thank you for sending it to us; we've been reading it over and over. Do you want it back today?"

"Oh no, keep it as long as you're using it," says the visitor. "And I saw a couple of other books on the table, too—*Snail Trails and Tadpole Tails* (Cohen, Tunick, & Seaberg, 1993), and a reference book on mollusks, I think?"

"Yes, I found that on my brother-in-law's bookshelves. The kids like the pictures a lot; they're mostly of ocean snails, and so they've started talking about the ocean. I guess it will soon be time to bring my scuba gear again." Sue is a scuba diver, and the ocean is a theme she regularly shares with children in her classes.

The visitor looks at the web some more. "I'm glad you included 'being gentle' and 'snails are different' and 'children are different,'" she says. "Those are certainly the things I heard you saying to the children, Sue, when they were handling the snails; 'Some of us like to touch snails, and some of us don't. There are big snails and little snails.' Nice."

Sue agrees. "It has been nice. Handwashing has been an outcome I certainly didn't think about at the beginning, but it's right there as something we talk about. Children get tired of adults' reminders to wash hands. Snail slime is a fine obvious reason to want to wash hands! And we all get to say 'Yuck' together as we scrub it off, but also to talk about why it's not yucky for the snails. They need that slime to keep from hurting themselves when they slide across rough places. The kids love that idea, even as they love saying, 'Yuck.'

Oh, and I looked on the Internet and found the book *Snail Trail* (Brown, 2000) at our public library. The illustrations are of a snail's-eye view moving up and down across a garden."

"So have all the children gotten into snails?" asks the visitor. "Not Evan," says Joyce. "Evan is my dinosaur boy. Let me show you his latest wonderful drawing."

The dinosaurs were indeed wonderful, and Joyce had put no pressure on Evan to give up dinosaurs because she was "doing snails." Projects in preschool are open-ended; like open-structure materials and teacher-established order in the material environment, projects are suggestions, not the only way to go. Whole-class projects on a topic come both from teachers' ideas and from some children's questions and initiative. Those children whose initiative is directed elsewhere need support in continuing to develop their own ideas, in play and in other symbolic activities. The teacher's intent is to generate enough ideas to catch the interest of all the children, diverse individuals that they are. She wants each child to discover the things that sustain his or her real interest, not to put aside personal passions for what we're all studying now. Sustained group projects in which everyone is expected to participate are more appropriate for school-age children when industry is the developmental task than for preschoolers who are practicing initiative (Erikson, 1950; Katz & Chard, 2000).

The web that the visitor encouraged the teachers to write down already existed in their heads as an invisible "web" of their own good ideas and their observations of children. Past their initial uncertainty in the face of a novel task, Sue and Joyce found it easy to make their ideas visible on paper. They aren't sure what to do with it next. Neither is the visitor, so they talk some more.

"Since you put up the web, has anyone noticed it?"

"Audrey has," says Joyce. "She recognized SNAILS, and then she asked me to read her the rest of it. I tried to read it to everyone at group time, too, but some of the children got too wiggly. Snails are great, but our 4-year-olds aren't ready for all those words. You know what Kaylin and Nancy did, though? They started copying the web, ignoring the words. Mrs. Serrano, my assisting teacher, walked by and asked `Is that a spider web? Where's the spider?' and Nancy said 'Make us a spider, please, please,' and Mrs. Serrano did. (I have tried to get her to stop drawing for the children, but she couldn't resist that please please!) It worked out fine, though, because they decided they wanted lots of baby spiders and began copying the big one and ended up with a great variety of their own creation."

"So you could add 'spiders' to the snail web, couldn't you? And Sue could think about adding ocean. Have any parents asked what you were doing?" The visitor is curious.

"No—but I've got it at the back of the room, and they don't usually come that far. That's an idea. I think I'll move it to the sign-in area and see if anyone comments," says Joyce.

"We put the web in Joyce's room because her kids are older," explains Sue.

Joyce continues, "I am excited to try a word wall in the room—I'll write some of the individual words from the snail web on cards backed with flannel, and we can hang them onto a big flannel board. I will wait to see what the kids notice and what kind of help they want to read them. Later I hope we'll add other words, ones that interest them from word lists for kindergarten-age kids."

"When I put up words, most of the threes don't notice them, unless it's their own names," says Sue. "Except Ernie—you saw him writing all over my note pad. He showed his mom the 'Snails—Ernie' words I put up near the terrarium, and she read them to him again. When my kids pay attention to writing, it's usually to me doing it, not to the words once they're done."

"Interesting. And that makes sense," says the visitor, "because most young children aren't yet ready for reading as a real task. What they do with reading and writing is just what they do with all the other adult behaviors they observe. They play them."

PLANNING FOR LITERACY AS A PLAYSCRIPT

Where adults read and write, at home and at preschool, children play reading and writing. Like other adult real-life behaviors, these behaviors have predictable scripts that children learn best by practicing them in their play. To read a book to a child, an adult chooses it from the shelf, holds it right side up, opens it from the front, turns the pages one by one, shows the pictures, and says the words. This sequence is obvious to an experienced reader, but young children are just learning it.

To encourage reading-as-play, a teacher reads—to the group of children and, when possible, to one or two children on her lap or snuggled close. She makes sure the books—the same books she reads aloud—are readily available to children during free play. She encourages books to be taken to different parts of the indoor and outdoor environment. There are books and magazines and catalogs in several different areas—next to the doll bed to be read at bedtime; in a cookbook in a kitchen cupboard with recipes, charts, and photos of food; in the "office," a picture dictionary; picture books on the live creatures in the natural world; and storybooks in a cozy area with pillows and stuffed animals where a child can relax and read to herself, her friend, her bear, or even a teacher. Like adult readers, children playing at being readers need control over a variety of reading materials with which they are free to settle down wherever they are comfortable.

This teacher supports reading-as-play by thoughtfully guiding the child's use of a computer.

Four-year-old George and I are sitting beside each other at a table. Relaxed in each other's company, we are drawing on lap-size chalkboards with chalk. George invents a game called "Guess what this is?" He draws, and I am supposed to guess. With each new drawing, George tells me a little story about it. One drawing I guess is "a car." George says it's a race car, and he has to work on it more. But he becomes frustrated, complaining that he can't remember the exact markings for his race car. (He wants to replicate the car's colors, shape, and numbering.) I invite George to go with me to the computer in the teachers' office so we can reference race cars on the Internet. With George sitting on my lap in the big teacher's chair, we search for several minutes. When we find the specific race car George wants, I print the page. Returning to the room with a paper copy of his race car, George settles down at the chalkboard to add important details to his drawing.

(Natasha daSilva, teacher)

To encourage writing-as-play, a teacher writes to communicate messages and remember obligations, in all the ways communication is called for naturally in the life of a classroom. He writes notes to parents, planning lists, lists for turns, "PLEASE SAVE" signs, and names on paintings. He calls casual attention to the fact that he is writing, and he uses large, clear print whenever practicable. He invites interested children to "write" for all these purposes, too, conveying his confidence in their ability to do so. In helping young kindergartners adjust to short whole-group circle time, he provides paper, pencils, and markers for children wishing to draw and write during circle, on their bellies on the floor, or on clipboards on their laps.

He thinks about the real-life settings in which people write and re-creates some of them in the play environment, stocking them with the tools people write with. And so there are pencils and pads of paper by the telephone, and a pad with a pencil on a string on the kitchen wall. He adds a receipt book and pens to the tools for fixing passing tricycles along the bike path, and next to the cash register in the store. There might be a doctor's office with prescription pads and patient charts, or a post office with envelopes and stamps and a mailbox, or an office like this one at Second Street preschool.

The teacher has just reorganized one corner of the room as an office, with a typewriter on a table, a keyboard, paper clips, recycled stamps, several older cell phones in a basket, staplers, and in the desk drawers, pens and pencils, used envelopes, Post-it notes, and several small spiral notebooks. Luz and Yolanda discover the office with delight; a volunteer mother puts paper in the typewriter for Luz. "Voy a trabajar [I'm going to work]," Yolanda announces. She picks up the phone. "Rring, rrring. Hello, hello . . . la senorita. Okay. Ahorita . . . voy, okay? Bye."

Another girl arrives. Yolanda and Luz tell her to go away, and she does. They continue their private conversation. Two other, smaller girls want to play in the office. "No! You can't come in here," says Yolanda, pushing her hands toward their faces. Holding hands, the little girls go to appeal to the teacher; seeing them go, Yolanda and Luz hide behind the table, yelling. The little girls do not return, and they come out again.

Animal crackers and juice have been put out on a nearby table for children who are interested in snack. Yolanda goes out for a plate of animal crackers; she brings them to the office. Sarah arrives and is accepted; she types and talks on the phone. Luz relaxes with the animal crackers, tucking her feet up under her. Yolanda looks for a wastebasket, and Sarah goes to find one, getting the teacher's permission to take it to the office. Yolanda is writing in a notebook; she tears out a couple of pages so Luz can write, too. Then they get on the phone. Apparently it's a message to go out. Yolanda gets her jacket, calls "Ándale, ándale!," and out of the office they go, giggling with the excitement of the play. As they run around the room, the teacher calls, "Sonando el teléfono," and back they go to answer the phone.

Luz and Sarah go off to the house area. Master player Yolanda follows her teacher's example: "El teléfono—anda rápido!" she calls, and back they come. Then all three are off again, this time to rescue the baby from a house on fire; several other children join the fire fighting, squirting pretend water. (They had recently gone on a class trip to the fire station.) When the excitement is over and it's clean-up time, Yolanda spends a long time putting everything away in its place, even lining up the typewriter carriage so it's just so.

As in much of real life, writing may be just one of the events in a complex play sequence. This office play included writing in a notebook and typing, coffee break, telephoning, and "This Is Our Private Office" and "Emergency" scripts, interweaving ideas, props, and people from several areas of the room. The teacher's planning set the stage; she permitted movement of people and things from one area to the other, intervening within the script (by suggesting that the phone was ringing) to forestall running around the room. The children built on the teacher's play ideas by introducing their own. Everyone was creatively involved in the emergences of meaningful curriculum.

PLAY-DEBRIEF-REPLAY

In play, we can try new things to see what will happen. In her book *Serious Players in the Primary Classroom* (2000), Selma Wassermann describes primary children's open-ended investigations of materials guided by teachers in a process she calls play-debrief-replay. The sequence is structured by the questions: What can you find out about this? (play) What happened? (debrief) Now what can you find out about this? (replay).

Play and *replay* are hands-on action and interaction with materials and other children. *Debrief* is conversation with the teacher and other children, which in the primary grades is sometimes carried on with the whole class. In many respects the process is like Paley's informal conversations with small groups of 3- to 5-year-olds about their play (1984, 1986a, 1988, 2004).

This model, we believe, can also be used by the teacher of young children in reflecting on her own process of emergent curriculum planning. In setting the stage, she is playing. What can I find out about the children if I get the bikes out, add water to the sand, put books next to the doll bed, increase the colors at the easel? In trying out new roles, she is playing. What can I find out if I ask children questions rather than putting them in time-out, if I join play as a visitor who has come to tea, if I draw a picture of a block construction and show it to the builder?

In reflecting on what she has found out, she is debriefing. What happened? she asks herself and, if she is fortunate, others. Adults, like children, learn more if they debrief in conversation with others. In too many programs, co-reflection is the "missing middle" in emergent curriculum planning (Stacey, 2009). In this book we have given examples of several such conversations (see Chapters 2, 5, and 7, as well as this chapter) carried on among students with a master teacher and between a visiting observer and a teacher or two.

Inventing a snails curriculum, Sue and Joyce shared their ideas and observations with each other. They were aware from the beginning that it offered possibilities for hands-on life science education, stimulating talk about how critters behave and the living conditions they need, and developing relationships and kinship with fragile living creatures (Curtis, 2010). But it hadn't occurred to Joyce that snails could make their own colored trails. (That was a child's idea; she dropped tempera paint on her paper and then got a snail to put in the color. Other children quickly noticed, and a whole new activity was born.) Nor had Joyce realized the extent to which her writing children's words would stimulate some children to practice writing for themselves. Sue had guessed that snails would interest the children but had not predicted that their interest would be sustained for more than a month, or that 3-year-olds might be interested in the act of writing. Making such discoveries along the way, teachers add to a curriculum web, modify a week's and, indeed, a year's plan, and keep observing, debriefing, and replaying, just as the children do.

Teacher educators are among the people who engage in debriefings with teachers. They would be well advised to follow Wassermann's and Paley's guidelines for asking genuine rather than loaded questions, the former leading teachers "to think and say more about their problems and possibilities," instead of giving answers that close the subject (Paley, 1986b, pp. 124–125). To help teachers understand what is happening and why, a curriculum director may paraphrase teachers' words or ask them to dig more deeply, engaging their thinking through responses that are respectful, attentive, and empowering (Wassermann, 2000). Teachers practicing with children have a privileged place to be researchers, where they learn by doing, through action, exploring theories and elaborating what they know. Emergent, responsive curriculum is the context that makes teaching as research possible (Rinaldi, 2006). Adults learn complex tasks like teaching "in much the same way as young children learn–through experimenting, problem-solving, talking with peers, asking questions, and making mistakes and reflecting on them" (Carter & Jones, 1990, pp. 28-29).

In trying out more ideas to support play and challenge children's thinking, the teacher is replaying: Now what can I find out? Through this process the curriculum keeps emerging, and the teacher, together with the children, keeps learning.

CHAPTER 9

Paying Attention to Play

How much attention do playing children need? All children in group settings need a stage manager—an adult attentive to the order and contents of the physical environment. Children's need for the direct involvement of an adult as player or mediator, however, decreases as their own ability to sustain play increases. The teacher of master players has less need to do, and more freedom to observe and plan, than the teacher of beginning players.

SUPPORTING CHILDREN WHO
HAVE NOT YET MASTERED PLAY

It isn't easy to pay attention to some children, those who have mastered, not play, but staying "invisible" (Rabiroff & Prescott, 1978). They need help in taking initiative, but often they remain unnoticed during playtimes—even though they may get considerable direct help at other times of the day.

At Second Street child care center, Becky, whom we first met in Chapter 1, is notably young among the 4-year-olds. At planning time her teacher focuses clearly on her to help her say and do the expected things. "Tell me where you're going to play. Can you say it louder so I can hear? Good!" At transitions the teacher often speaks Becky's name to remind her of the next task to be accomplished. She's thoughtful about paying attention to Becky outside of playtime.

During playtime most of the 4-year-olds in this class are assertive and full of play ideas; it would be hard for the adults to miss what they're doing. "Teacher, look!" is frequently heard, as the children make sure their play is being noticed and appreciated. Their playscripts are full of action: We're Galloping on Our Horses, It's Vanessa's Birthday and She's Five, Superman to the Rescue. Surrounded by all this action, teachers of 4-year-olds may get out of the habit of noticing and responding to small beginnings, which the adults working with young 3-year-olds next door do all the time.

Here is Becky outside one day.

Stephanie and Vanessa are busy in the sand. Becky wanders in their direction, carrying a pail and shovel. As she steps into the sand, the girls run off. She sees a dump truck and settles down with it, using her shovel to fill it with dirt. After a while she gets up, holding the truck, and turns it sideways to drive it along the whole length of the vertical wall. Then she drives it back to the sand, where Richard is now playing.

Becky plunks down in front of Richard, saying something softly. She digs a shovelful of sand and holds it up at an angle, watching the sand slowly run out of it. She watches Richard pouring sand into a funnel. She tries to take the funnel, but Richard holds on; neither of them says anything.

Becky finds the dump truck again and starts driving it, this time along the narrow concrete edge of the sand area. She moves behind the swings, where two adults are pushing children. One of them is counting as she pushes. Becky stands up, holding her truck. "Look, wheels. One, two, three, four," she says softly. No one hears her. Clean-up time is announced. "Becky, let's go," says the assistant teacher, taking her by the hand in a friendly way.

Becky tried a few small beginnings that might have developed into shared playscripts if anyone had helped. I'm Driving My Truck; How Can I Pour Sand?; One, Two, Three, Four Wheels—rudimentary ideas, certainly, but they have possibilities. But the adults were occupied; the refrain, "Teacher, help me," is hard to ignore. It's important, though, to divide adult energy between response to children's requests and noticing those children who haven't learned how to ask for what they need.

The teacher was quick to acknowledge, when asked by an observer, that Becky was a child who might benefit from special attention during free play. On another visit, the observer saw the teacher sit down in the sand near Becky, who welcomed the opportunity to tell about her kitty at home, and then started finding rocks for her teacher: Two baby rocks. One big rock. The teacher was appreciative, and together they found a whole family of rocks.

On this occasion, no other children were nearby. On the earlier day, an attentive adult might have been able to initiate social play by taking on the role of mediator, stage manager, or player—perhaps like this.

Teacher as Mediator. Had an adult been nearer the sand, she might have offered assistance when Becky tried unsuccessfully to take the funnel. "Becky, you would like the funnel. Richard, you have a funnel. Becky would like a funnel, too. What do you think we could do about that?" Depending on various factors, including Richard's willingness or unwillingness to share, the availability of extra funnels, and the adult's ideas for complicating play, parallel or cooperative dramatic play might have been an outcome of this intervention, giving Becky a place in the play life of the group.

Teacher as Stage Manager. Adults, with less at stake in play, can remain more alert than children to all the resources of the environment. Looking quickly around, an adult might have spotted an extra funnel, two cups, and several pails. Gathering them up, she could sit in the sand near Becky and Richard. "I found another funnel. Becky, would you like a funnel? I found some cups, too. Richard, do you need a cup? Becky, do you need a cup? What else do you need to pour sand?" By adding materials and including both children in her offer of them, an adult can suggest the possibility of playing together while adding the reassurance of her presence.

Teacher as Player. An adult can offer props and leave their use up to children, or can model their use as well. This adult, having found more sand toys, might have refrained from comment and simply settled down close to the children to play with them. She would respond to any show of interest with willingness to share. She might pour with one cup while putting the other cup strategically between herself and Becky. By her actions as well as her presence, she would highlight the possibilities of sand play and invite social interaction and pretending: "Would you like a drink of my chocolate milk?"

It is at least as important to respond to children's initiative in play as it is to reinforce their desired behaviors in other situations. Abdou's teacher, in Chapter 8, sometimes has difficulty finding desired behaviors to reinforce for him, but she manages to acknowledge all his play discoveries even while fending off his intrusions into others' space. Abdou, of course, is a very visible child, guaranteeing himself adult response of some kind. Becky is one of the quiet ones, capable of making herself invisible.

SUPPORTING MASTER PLAYERS

Adults interested in the scripts children play find it easy to pay attention to master players. They're the children whose words delight our ears, whose skill in negotiation enables them to sustain play without our help, whose creativity in dealing with fantasy, friendship, and fairness–that trilogy of preschool priorities (Paley, 1986b)–confirms our *image of the child* as "competent, active, critical" (Rinaldi, 2006, p. 83), and confirms that we are, after all, good teachers of young children. For nearly an hour one day, these 4-year-old master players placed no demands on their teacher; he was free to enjoy, to observe, and to write down some of their memorable words to share later with parents and other staff.

Outdoors at Live Oak child care center a split-level water table—homemade, with cutout holes to insert plastic dish tubs—has been filled with goop, a cornstarch-

and-water mixture. Extra bowls, spoons, and trowels are at hand. Paula, Dena, and Megan are busy mixing; they have added leaves and dirt to the goop.

PAULA (*stirring competently*): We're making chocolate.
DENA (*bringing more dirt*): This is chocolate. Stir it up.
PAULA: We're making cookies and cream.
DENA: Ice cream. Please can I have a cone?

She presents a funnel to Paula, who fills it generously. Someone adds water to the mixture. "Don't," Paula yells, and the child, intimidated, retreats. Dena has finished her ice cream. Now she arrives with a cup of water to add to her friend's mixture.

DENA (*dumping water*): Dumping. Lots of goosh.
PAULA: No more. It's getting too gooey, right? We have a magic. We're magic witches of the East, right? She's never gonna learn about us. She'll die.
MEGAN (*arriving*): We'll be the fairest one in the world. (*She starts stirring in the other tub.*)
DENA (*running back and forth between the two tubs, with handfuls of mixture for each*): We're gonna have our magic. This is our magic food for Snow White.
MEGAN: We don't blow hair out of our nose. The witch doesn't blow hair out of her nose. How about, we don't blow hair out of our nose, but our mother does?

When master players engage in messy play with cornstarch and leaves, dirt and water, they aren't making messes, they're magic potions or ice cream. Like the real cooks they watch at home, who magically transform varied ingredients into edible food, master players are remaking the natural world. Transformation, making something into something else, is a basic theme in both science and mythology. Transformation has particular importance for young children, who, as theories of cognitive development suggest, are learning that materials, objects, and people can have more than one attribute at the same time.

We have known young children who are passionate about Transformers action figures (based on superhero science fiction themes), and we wonder: Do Transformers toys fascinate because with a few twists and turns of body parts or machinery parts the toy is completely different? Grasping transformation is key to understanding reversibility, a necessary concept in understanding quantity and parts-and-wholes (Clements & Sarama, 2009). It is a key to literacy as well. *The hundred languages* is a metaphor for the multiple ways an idea can be represented meaningfully and for the interconnectedness of modes of expression (Rinaldi, 2006). One day a child may take a marker and fill her paper with high-energy swirls and zigzags. Later she might request a scarf and invent a wild dance for you. Another time she may ask how to write the words "scary thunderstorm." All three representations of thunderstorm are equally powerful. There's an interconnectedness among all forms of expression—each building upon the others, all of them enriching and deepening the child's understanding of a concept. All children are capable of expressing ideas in multiple ways, provoking us to question why schools emphasize only oral and written language.

A teacher who knows something about cognitive development theory is reassured, watching these children at play: They're really learning something; they're not "just playing." They are thriving in the learning environment he has prepared for them. He can use his observations to reassure their parents, too, explaining why this play is developmentally important. Master players free a teacher to move into the roles of scribe, assessor, and communicator—appreciating children's skills in play and language and representing these on paper to be communicated to the other adults who have particular interest in these children's growth, and to the children themselves.

Teacher as Scribe. Taking notes as he watched this play, the teacher knew that these older 4-year-olds were becoming actively interested in reading and writing, and guessed that they might respond to a "chalk talk" about their play.

Because snack at Live Oak is a choice in the middle of playtime, children don't all arrive or leave at once. Predictably, Megan, Dena, and Paula arrived together. The teacher had moved an easel near the snack table, and as they ate, he began to draw. They were immediately interested. "That's our water table," said Megan, as it took shape on the paper. "Who's that?" (see Figure 9.1a).

"Who do you think it is?" asked the teacher as he kept drawing.

"It's not me," said Megan decidedly. "My hair is real long. That silly person's got no hair!"

"It's Dena," teased Paula.

"It's not!" screamed Dena.

"Shall I give it some hair?" said the teacher, adding lots. "Now who could it be?"

Conversation continued as the teacher finished drawing people and began to write words (see Figure 9.1b). "That says 'Paula,'" announced Paula, proudly. "You wrote my name. What does that say?"

The drawing stayed on the easel, generating interest from other children as well as return visits from the girls to read names, add features to the figures, and make drawings of their own on new sheets of paper. The play itself resumed after snack, with elaboration of the Snow White theme and "lots of goosh." Imaginative language often grows out of messing for the sheer joy of it; both are open-ended, spontaneous explorations of unlimited possibilities.

FIGURE 9.1. "Who do you think it is?"

(a)

Paula said, "We're making chocolate."
Paula said, "We're making cookies and cream."
Dena said, "We're making ice cream."
Dena said, "We're making goosh."
Dena said, "We're making magic food for Snow White."
Megan said, "We'll be the fairest one in the world."

(b)

Teacher as Assessor and Communicator. The chalk-talk conversation enabled the teacher to make an informal assessment of each child's interest and skills in literacy. He noted that all three girls could read their own and each other's names, and were interested in the other words on the paper. Megan promptly recognized the water table; later in the day, she included it in a drawing of her own, surrounded by long-haired girls. Paula covered a page with her name, accurately printed. Dena's rainbow painting had D's and e's flying in its sky. "That's a D," she said to no one in particular. Then she looked at it again, attached another D, and added antennae and spots to make it into a butterfly. The teacher, as interested in creative thinking as he is in literacy development, made a note of that, too, and showed it to Dena's father at the end of the day. The girls spontaneously showed their parents both the teacher's drawing and their own, and communication flourished. "What did you do at school today?" Here it is!

Teacher as Planner. The teacher, in the role of planner, will ask the girls their ideas for elaborating the play. As an adult enjoys children's imaginativeness, he can be imaginative, too. Are there ways in which he might extend and further enrich this already rich play by choosing an idea from it that sparks his thinking or by adding materials, conversation, storytelling, or the written word? He wants to ask the girls their ideas for elaborating the play. How about adding cedar shavings or beach pebbles in the water table? How about making real chocolate or real ice cream or cookies? How about transforming the chalk-talk into a flannel board activity that children could repeat on their own?

This teacher got excited by his flannel board idea. He cut out child shapes in several shades of brown, tan, and peach to match the varied skin colors of the children in the class. He cut out a couple of water tables, a climber, swings on a frame, six bikes, several tables, and chairs. He added additional scraps that looked to him like nothing in particular but would probably look like something to the children. He decided to tell a flannel board story about children playing outside, make the materials available during free-play time, and see what happened. Watching master players and responding to their ideas and demands, a teacher becomes a master player, too.

TEACHER ROLE DEVELOPMENT

Like children at play, adults who work with children grow in their mastery of role behaviors. Developmentally oriented teacher education offers many opportunities to practice these roles and reflect on one's performance. But many staff members in preschool and kindergarten programs begin their work without such practice. Some have been trained in primary education, which in practice does not value play. Others bring goodwill and life experience but little training; their competence is based on past experience with children (including parenting) or on being in touch with the child in themselves (Jones, 1984). On a teaching team they can contribute different perspectives. For example, parents who have been at home with children for a few years returning to teach in early childhood may bring home management skills and resourcefulness to the larger stage of a preschool; drawing on these skills, they get satisfaction from creating figure-ground relationships, cultivating a garden, and repairing program equipment. Many young adults trying out child care as an entry-level job are especially good players; they can be encouraged to provision imaginatively for play as well as participate in it.

Stage manager is the most basic of the roles, to be mastered by all staff. In a well-ordered, well-provisioned environment with plenty of time for play, most children will be able to create and sustain their own play as they have always done in homes and neighborhoods. Play in itself meets many of young children's growth needs. It is a self-teaching, self-healing process.

Fortunately, stage management seems to be the easiest role to learn. Nearly all adults are experienced in organizing and maintaining living spaces and time schedules for themselves; this experience transfers directly to the preschool. And it is easier and more appropriate to learn to manipulate environments rather than to manipulate children. If things aren't going well, let's think about how we could move the furniture, change the schedule, add props for play, rethink our organization of learning centers (Carter, 2001; Greenman, 1988; Kritchevsky & Prescott, 1969). We can criticize how the stage set works without criticizing how the adults or children act. Working behind the scenes, we can experiment with space, time, and materials without having to change our interactions with children during the time we're onstage. Sensibly, developmentally oriented early childhood curricula begin with the concrete, hands-on arrangement of space and materials (Dodge, 1993; Hohmann, Banet, & Weikart, 1979).

Mediator, a necessary role if children are to grow in problem-solving skills, employs power *for* rather than power *on.* It is unfamiliar to many adults, who bring to children's conflicts either an inclination to withdraw from their expression of strong feelings, or a no-nonsense power *on* approach: "I'm the grown-up here and I am in charge." To help children find their own solutions rather than impose an adult solution seems to undermine many adults' sense of order, control, and the rightness of things. They believe in teaching obedience rather than critical thinking.

Power *on* solutions have the virtue of familiarity for many children, and security; it is clear that this grown-up knows and enforces the rules. But such solutions, unlike those mediated with children, interrupt play and the development of autonomy. Mediation skills can be discussed and practiced within the context of program policy that defines conflict resolution as a goal. They are not difficult to learn for those who believe in their importance.

Player is a role that comes naturally to adults in touch with the child in themselves. In families, adults play with children in a variety of ways: conversation, roughhousing, make-believe, games with rules, storytelling, spontaneous games (Segal & Adcock, 1981). Such mutual play builds relationships and contributes to children's play skills as well.

We have, however, observed many thoughtful teachers who remain on the periphery of children's play, paying attention but not participating. Some of them, when asked, explain that they simply aren't comfortable playing with children. Others have made a deliberate choice based on their feeling that adult involvement undermines the initiative of children at play. As we discussed in Chapter 4, both the age of the children and their familiarity with the culture of the preschool seem to be significant considerations here; thoughtful adults intervene more readily in the play of children for whom the preschool or kindergarten is a new and unfamiliar place. They move toward the periphery as children become masters of play in this setting. Player is a useful but not necessary role, we have come to believe. Adults can share play ideas with children through props and conversation as well as through playing themselves.

Scribe, even if it is an unfamiliar role to preschool teachers, seems nonetheless to be a welcome one, especially for adults who fail to see much value in "just playing" and who are invested in their "teaching" role. We have watched a teacher assistant, whose special joy is in the adult-directed craft activities she meticulously prepares, as she discovers that writing down the children's talk about their work can provide impressively diverse content for her bulletin boards. While she is busy writing, the children have more freedom to create without her direction. Adults often find it easier to write down children's answers to questions asked at group time or to record their dictated stories than to capture their language during play; the latter task requires more challenging observation skills. But the role definition, "teachers are people who write down children's words," seems generally to be a congenial one.

If staff or teachers with minimal background in early childhood education assume the roles of assessor, communicator, and planner, they are likely to fall back on inappropriate, traditional versions of the school game.

It is through direct teaching and questioning—"today we're learning the let-ter B"–rather than planning for and observing play that many teachers keep themselves accountable. Accountability is important. But in early childhood programs, it is accountability for play that matters.

A PLACE IN THE WORLD FOR CHILDREN

Because play is self-sustaining, competent adults in the roles of stage man-ager and mediator will sustain a nurturing environment for young children in the short run. However, all the roles become important when teachers as-sume the care and education of young children over the long run. They are working in partnership with parents, who are already involved in the same roles at home.

Good parents assume these roles intuitively because they are invested in their child (Katz, 1980). They repeat her funny sayings to Grandma, take her picture and put it in the family scrapbook, and show her how to write the name they call her by. They plan family activities that include her, and special events for her because she's special to them. They are observant of her growth in competence because they are invested in her accomplishments as mirrors of their success in parenting. For *personal* reasons rooted in the meaning of their life as a family, parents document and plan for their child's growth, giving her and themselves a firm sense of their shared past and fu-ture. She is theirs, and what she does matters very much to them.

Professionals are motivated not by their love for a particular child but by their skills and commitment to the importance of developmentally appropri-ate experiences for all children (Katz, 1980). A child in an early childhood program is a member of a group of children that has no permanence, no past and future, in which he is no longer so special. While a few programs admi-rably attempt to compensate for this impermanence by keeping a group of children together with the same adults for several years, or by other variants of "family grouping," the realities of staff and family mobility create frequent separations and losses.

Professional rather than personal responsibility provides the continuity in children's experience in early childhood programs. Children becoming master players are occupied in representing, in order to understand, the con-tinuing stories of their own lives. Under the conditions of modern society, most children need help from adults in doing so. In traditional societies the play of young children often has been ignored by adults, and children have been let be–typically under conditions of adequate space and time, avail-ability of natural materials, and a wide-age community of children for whom the observable work and ceremonial world of adults is a ready source of play themes. In such a setting the stage for children's play is set by the community as a whole, and play is facilitated by adults' leaving it alone.

In some homes and neighborhoods, similar play conditions can be found even in modern society. But increasingly they have become the exception rather than the rule. And so we have teachers and other specialized caregivers responsible for the daily lives of many children under school age and faced with defining suitable roles for adult behavior in preschool group settings. Further, children and adults alike are living in a diverse, complex, and rapidly changing world in which the ability to define and solve new problems is a crucial skill to be developed. It is no longer enough for young children to imitate the behavior of their elders in order to grow up competent.

When parents care for children at home, they have many other tasks to accomplish as well, thus ensuring children some freedom from constant supervision. In out-of-home child care settings the adults are constrained, often legally, to watch children every minute in order to be responsible for their safety. Simply babysitting young children, while doing nothing else of importance, is a task that fails to challenge the competence or sense of duty of most responsible adults. And so they look for other roles. Of these the most familiar, acquired through their own school experience, is teacher-as-teller—someone who gives information and orders to (hopefully) quiet and obedient children. True, some adults find themselves engaged in frequent struggles with noisy and innovative children, but these struggles help to justify the importance of their work; they are establishing civility and order in the face of chaos and anarchy. Teacher-as-disciplinarian is another familiar role that goes with the territory in schools.

All the roles we have described in this book are less familiar. They reflect modern theoretical views, rather than traditional commonsense views, of how children learn. They are, for the most part, professional rather than technical roles, requiring continual exercise of judgment rather than mere carrying out of standardized, trainable procedures. These roles call for skills in dramaturgy, mediation, observation, assessment, and creative planning. They ask adults to take the play of young children seriously, while being playfully responsive to its unfolding.

Parents' competence in childrearing comes directly out of the relationship: Because this child is mine and I love her, I will do my very best for her. This motivation for competence is largely absent in people caring for other people's children in groups. A popular alternative approach to competence, reflecting behaviorist thinking, has been to try to train caregivers as technicians. "Teacher-proof curricula" comparable to those that pervade elementary education (in spite of the professional certification of elementary teachers, as Kamii, 1985, has pointed out) can be found in abundance on the display tables at any early childhood conference.

For several reasons, we believe this approach to be inadequate. One reason is the very limitation of training opportunities and the rapid turnover of child care workers. Technical knowledge takes time to acquire. A second, more significant reason reflects a point made by Jean Baker Miller (1976)– that there are tasks (historically, these are usually women's tasks) that are too variable to be approached technically. Like the high-level professions, they require the continual exercise of judgment. One such task is childrearing.

Third, as Nel Noddings (2003) has described, the ethical imperative underlying both childrearing and early childhood education is *caring*. Adults who choose to work with young children are, for the most part, people who enjoy children and who believe, on the basis of their own positive or negative experience, that the quality of childhood matters. In this experience lies the source of the empathy that is essential to caring and that supports an appreciation of the importance of play in the lives of young children. Young children at play are happy and lively, qualities that such adults appreciate. The creation of a community of caring people, big and little, is the most important goal in child care. People who care about each other help each other grow and learn (New, 1990).

The early childhood professionals on a program staff as mentors, advisors, directors, or pedagogistas (Edwards, Gandini, & Forman, 1998) can coach all the teacher's roles, while sharing responsibility for assessing, communicating, and planning. In most programs they offer leadership and dialogue to a staff team with varying levels of experience and training. We believe that the best guidance they can give to all staff is, *Try not to interrupt play*. It will make most sense if the advice-giver is on the spot while children are playing, to name the play, describe it in detail, and represent it for both adults and children in a variety of ways that enable the adults to slow down, pay attention, and appreciate the importance of children's learning through play.

CHAPTER 10

A Sense of
the Past and the Future

Play is not simply a tool that adults can manipulate to hurry children toward "school readiness." Although the developmental theories of Vygotsky, Erikson, and Piaget have given solid response to the question, "What is play good for?" children undertake play for its own sake. Play is the natural activity of early childhood—what children do best.

Monighan-Nourot (1990), reviewing the historical development of rationales for play in early childhood education, distinguishes between the philosophical/moral rationale, which "rests on the belief in the inherent value of the childhood activity of play in and of itself and represents a humanistic attitude in protecting the rights of the vulnerable and malleable child," and the instrumental rationale, which demands evidence that play has future value for the child and society (p. 60). Instrumental justifications abound, she comments, "in the research literature generated by Piagetian notions of the contribution of play to development" (p. 77). In our view, looking at the place of play in a developmental framework, as we have done in Chapter 1, offers more than instrumental justification for children's play. Development is a history, a story; the human life cycle is a pattern, a narrative in which each chapter has its own significance and each player discovers her own play.

> In the days when the Eldest Magician was getting Things ready, he told all the Animals that they could come out and play. And the Animals said, "O Eldest Magician, what shall we play at?" and he said, "I will show you." He took the Elephant—All-the-Elephant-there-was—and said, "Play at being an Elephant," and All-the-Elephant-there-was played. He took the Beaver—All-the-Beaver-there-was—and said, "Play at being a Beaver," and All-the-Beaver-there-was played. (Kipling, 1978/1902, pp. 143–144)

Children play at being a Child. Play is their major form of representation; it is a necessary stage in development. Looking at behavior developmentally gives it a past and a future. Children are learners as well as doers. What they're learning by playing is mastery of play, an important mode of being in the world that will serve them all their lives as well as here and now. Play is children's *optimal experience.* In play children achieve a sense of *flow,* a temporary state where mind and body are completely engaged in an activity and where external conditions are forgotten. "Optimal experiences add up to a sense of mastery—a sense of participation in determining the content of life—that comes as close to happiness as anything else we can conceivably imagine" (Csikszentmihalyi, 1990, p. 4).

THE LOGIC OF HUMAN RELATIONSHIPS

Most educators, even in early childhood, are more interested in teaching their adult ways of thinking about the world to children than in exploring the child's own meanings. Professionals in any field are apt to behave in this way, striving to teach the student or client the professional's language rather than to learn the language of the other (Watzlawick, Weakland, & Fisch, 1974).

Children's meanings are embedded in their experiences. But as Margaret Donaldson (1978) has pointed out, our technological society places the highest value on the capacity for *disembedded* thinking: "The better you are at tackling problems without having to be sustained by human sense the more likely you are to succeed in our educational system" (pp. 77–78). Disembedded thinking is objective,

> abstracted from all basic purposes and feelings and endeavors. It is totally cold-blooded. In the veins of 3-year-olds, the blood still runs warm.
>
> This is in no way to suggest that the ability to deal, in cold blood, with problems of an abstract and formal nature is unimportant. It is immensely important. Much that is distinctly human and highly to be valued depends upon it. And young children are bad at it. (pp. 17–18)

Before they can become good at it, however, they need to put first things first—to learn about "basic human purposes and feelings and endeavors." The play in which young children invest so much of their cognitive and affective energy is not primarily concerned with problems of an abstract and formal nature, with the classification of colors, numbers, and spatial relationships. Imaginative play is the medium that, according to Vygotsky (1978), frees young children's embedded knowing. It is the arena where children are no longer bound by the immediate perception of things and come to rely instead on the expression of symbolic meanings. Imaginative play is "the zone of proximal development" where children can perform "a head taller" than they are capable of under normal circumstances because the context is appropriate to childhood forms of knowing.

Young children's primary concern is *human* relationships. *Daddy, Mommy, sister,* and *baby* are understood before *bigger, big, little,* and *littlest. Home,* an emotionally laden image, is understood before *house,* a building where people live together. Children's play integrates feelings and facts; it is both art and science.

> The classroom has all the elements of theater, and the observant, self-examining teacher will not need a drama critic to uncover character, plot and meaning. We are, all of us, the actors trying to find the meaning of the scenes in which we find ourselves. The scripts are not yet fully written, so we must listen with curiosity and great care to the main characters who are, of course, the children. (Paley, 1986b, p. 131)

Play can best be understood through skilled teachers' stories of children's play and conversations about play (Clemens, 1983; Griffin, 1982; Hawkins, 1974; Paley, 1984, 1986a, 1988, 1990, 2004; Reynolds & Jones, 1997). As Coles (1989) and Egan (1989) insist, stories are often more effective conveyors of human knowledge than scientific analyses are.

> We need, for the educational benefit of children, to reconstruct our curricula and teaching methods in light of a richer image of the child as an imaginative as well as a logico-mathematical thinker. What we call imagination is also a tool for learning—in the early years perhaps the most energetic and powerful one. (Egan, 1989, p. 17)

In their accounts of children's apparent "illogic," sensitive observers uncover the emotional logic of their stories and dramatic play.

> "Frederick, I'm curious about something I heard you say in the doll corner yesterday. You said your mother doesn't have birthdays any more." (Frederick knows my tendency to begin informal conversations in this manner, and he responds immediately).
>
> "She doesn't. How I know is no one comes to her birthday and she doesn't make the cake."
>
> "Do you mean she doesn't have a birthday party?"
>
> "No. She really doesn't have a birthday."
>
> "Does she still get older every year?"
>
> "I think so. You know how much old she is? Twenty-two."
>
> "Maybe you and your dad could make her a birthday party."
>
> "But they never remember her birthday and when it's her birthday

they forget when her birthday comes, and when her birthday comes they forget how old she is because they never put any candles. So how can we say how she is old?"

"The candles tell you how old someone is?"

"You can't be old if you don't have candles."

"Frederick, I'll tell you a good thing to do. Ask mother to have a cake and candles. Then she'll tell you when her birthday is."

"No. Because, see, she doesn't have a mother so she doesn't have a birthday."

"You think because your grandma died your mother won't have any more birthdays?"

"Right. Because, see, my grandma borned her once upon a time. Then she told her about her birthday. Then every time she had a birthday my grandma told. So she knew how many candles to be old." (Paley, 1986b, p. 125)

This is a competent 4-year-old figuring out the world. Is it any wonder that, as Paley says, "'Birthday' is a curriculum in itself" (p. 126), which someone in the group plays out every day? By listening for the "answers I could not myself invent" (p. 125), Paley opens windows for herself and her readers into the meaning-filled worlds of the preschool child and offers a model for other teachers having conversations with children.

Play is storytelling. It is both concrete and intelligible to adults who take the trouble to "learn the language of the other"–the playing child. A teacher who has taken a great deal of trouble to learn this language explains, "'Pretend' often confuses the adult, but it is the child's real and serious world, the stage upon which any identity is possible and secret thoughts can be safely revealed" (Paley, 1990, p. 7). Young children's greatest strength in the acquisition of knowledge is their passion for play. In stark contrast, Piaget suggested that children confronting reality develop creative thinking to escape from the oppressive nature of reality. Educators inspired by the pedagogy of Reggio Emilia's municipal preprimary schools disagree with this limited view of play. Carlina Rinaldi (2006) writes that play is an essential element of the human being. Play and learning are mutually supporting, and if play is taken away from children and adults, the possibility for learning is diminished. Do educators, accountable for learning in classrooms, make equal effort to recognize and legitimate children's creative processes? Creativity " . . . requires a context that allows it to exist, to be expressed, to become visible. In schools, creativity should have the opportunity to be expressed in every place and in every moment. What we hope for is creative learning and creative teachers, not simply a 'creativity hour'" (pp. 119–120).

Teachers who have faith in the process of development can capitalize on it, building on developmental strengths rather than reacting to deficiencies. We are not simply advocating the maturationist, "leave them alone to grow" view that Kohlberg (DeVries & Kohlberg, 1990) has labeled *romantic.* As we have made clear throughout this book, teachers have important roles in children's play. Growth is an interactive process. Children learn through adult guidance as well as through their self-directed encounters with the world. Such guidance, we believe, should be directed toward the mutual creation of an adult-child culture in which meanings are shared.

STORIES, IMAGES, AND THE CREATION OF CULTURE

The bridge from embedded toward disembedded thinking is best built through stories and images rather than through abstractions. Bridge-building should begin with the child's personal concerns, a beginning that asks the teacher to use power *with* rather than the consistent power *for* of the cognitively oriented teacher (see Chapter 5). As observer, player, and asker-of-questions, the power *with* teacher looks and listens for the "answers I could not myself invent" (Paley, 1986b, p. 125), for the "key words" and images that erupt from the volcano of the child's emotionally laden experiences (Ashton-Warner, 1963).

Cognitive theory and practice give priority to the development of logical reasoning, viewing intuition and the arts as precursors to logical and scientific thought. Psychodynamic theory, which recognizes the threats that anxiety introduces into the growth process (Erikson, 1950; Maslow, 1962), supports a view of the arts as creative, complementary modes of thought that serve adults as well as children (DeVries & Kohlberg, 1990). The arts create the power of magic, essential for dealing with the things that go bump in the night. All cultures use magic in the face of the unknown. The arts, in the hands of both children and teachers, provide the creative vent for the child's volcanic energy (Ashton-Warner, 1963). Teachers of young children can support children's play by becoming *keepers of metaphor*—both source and recorder of stories and images.

In all cultures, people who share experiences create metaphors—stories, songs, dances, and visual images—in order to remember their experiences, give them new meanings, and build community through their sharing. In Bolivia, for example, early childhood educators are exploring ways to sustain creativity in the lives of children and educators. Despite extreme poverty, this work is supported because families are eager to participate; the natural wonders of the environment are the mountains, rivers, and forests, and Bolivians have language, traditions, legends, songs, dances, and art.

Where we did not have tables, we had flat areas of earth; where we did not have pencils, we had branches and charcoal; where we did not have white papers, we had old newspapers and flat stones; where we did not have colours, we had plants, flowers, fruits and soil; and where we did not have teachers, we had mothers and young community volunteers. The constant was, however, that we always have children who want to live, to learn, and to dream. (Salazar & Schulze, 2010, p. 4)

Among the several basic needs of young children, one is *a sense of the past and the future* (Jones & Prescott, 1982). Children need to know that they have a place in the world, that they matter, and that they will be cared for. Families convey this knowledge through stories and images: "When you were a baby. . ."; "When Mommy was a little girl. . ."; "When we go to Grandma's, we'll. . ."; "When it's your birthday. . . ." Are digital photos displayed on screens as conducive to shared memories as hand-held paper photos used to be? Eating supper together at a local restaurant, Mom handed the cell phone to her daughter. Three-year-old Rachel aptly opened the photos area and scrolled through many photos loaded there, while Grandma admired and described them: Here you are feeding the ducks; remember Mommy's picnic lunch; Daddy and you flew the box kite; Uncle Eric took you wading.

People who live together need to create a culture together, in order to make connections with one another and assure themselves that their time together is of value. Even preschool children in child care are occupied with creating a peer culture, often focused on the stories and images from their common experience with entertainment media: TV, video, electronic learning games, toys, popular fast food outlets, and movies. For older children, peer culture that adults may find offensive supports the process of growth toward independence. But 3-, 4-, and 5-year-olds aren't ready for independence; they need adults to take care of them and to share meanings with them. Young children's takeover of media dramas more appropriate for older children distances them from adults too soon, in a society in which children leave home for day care younger and younger and are thus physically distanced from the people with whom their deepest meanings are shared.

TEACHER AS KEEPER OF METAPHOR

The ways in which teachers and caregivers can establish metaphoric connections with young children include (1) joining their media play, (2) introducing alternative dramatic scripts, and (3) representing children's stories, images, and play in new modes.

Joining Children's Media Play

I explained to the children in my class that I wanted to understand more about why children like to play Teenage Mutant Ninja Turtles and chase games and that I wanted to interview them individually during play time and tape record their answers to some questions about this kind of play. I had 30 volunteers the first day!

I responded with curiosity and openness to the many "lessons" the children gave me. I watched the television show and conversed with the children about past episodes. The children's active play seemed to change almost immediately after I shared my interest in "Turtle culture." The children no longer took on a clandestine manner as they chased each other on the playground; instead, they yelled to me as they ran past, "Jacob is Shredder and we're all Donatello chasing him!" I could then respond in the correct lingo, "Cowabunga, Dudes!"

The aggressiveness of the play lessened. As I watched more closely, I saw that most of the kicking and karate chopping was indeed an attempt at "fake fighting." Unfortunately, the amount of necessary skill in controlling such gross motor movements is not well developed in kindergarten, so injuries occurred. With the advent of the Ninja Turtles movie, I was able to introduce the concept of stuntmen and women who practice very carefully planned fake fights. A simple reminder of "Fight like they did in the movie" was all that was needed most of the time. (Gronlund, 1992, pp. 22–23)

Gronlund's experiment with her kindergarten class, undertaken out of her concern that "the children's play did not appear imaginative, rich, or inventive" (p. 21), followed the suggestion of Carlsson-Paige and Levin (2006) that adults can respond to, challenge, and complicate children's war and weapons play. The children's eagerness to include an interested teacher suggests that they do not seek to be left on their own with media stereotypes; it is our distaste that leaves them there. This teacher's willingness to exercise power *with* gave her access to the peer culture and thus expanded her opportunities to teach.

Introducing Alternative Dramatic Scripts

I begin by telling the story over several times. Very quickly most children pick up the progression and begin to join the chorus of "Who's that trip-trapping over my bridge?" "It's me, the littlest Billy Goat Gruff."

When the children are all familiar with the structure of the tale, I ask if they would like to act it out. There is an immediate wave of "I want to be _____." I explain that we will act the play many times until everyone has had a chance to play all the parts he wants. (Howarth, 1988, pp. 160–161)

Howarth (1988, 1989) introduces fairytale dramatization into the classroom as an alternative to the "hard, indigestible, violent stereotypes, particularly male," that are children's diet in the mass media. Fairy tales have historical rather than commercial roots; they have stood the test of time. They are found in all cultures, and the tales selected by a teacher should make connections with the family cultures of the children in her class, as well as broadening children's experience through familiarity with tales from other heritages.

"As in all great dramas, the themes in fairy tales echo humanity's deepest concerns and fears, thereby facilitating each child's growth and development" (Howarth, 1988, p. 173). They expose children to the "'archetypal images we all need to confront,'" offering potential situations and characters to be incorporated into children's playing out of the issues in their own lives. These issues are not all easy ones; good and evil are present in children's lives, even the best of them.

> We do not limit the colors we offer them with which to paint; we encourage their experimentation with art media, enriching their environments with texture and shape. But we are often afraid to recognize that a child's life is made up of both light and dark feelings, which she also needs to name and utilize. How can she know that humankind has experienced all these same feelings for millennia? (p. 182)

Stories told and books read to young children should be more than factual; they should be dramatically memorable, with potential for being played, talked about, assimilated into one's own language. "Who's that trip-trapping over my bridge?" said the great big Troll. "You monkeys, you. You give me back my caps" (Slobodkina, 1947). But Pierre said, "I don't care" (Sendak, 1962).

Representing Children's Stories, Images, and Play in New Modes

"Once upon a time," said Joan to her small class of 3-year-olds, whom she had called into a snug circle as their "going camping" play was coming to an end, and before clean-up time, "there were one, two, three, four, five, six, seven, eight children who went camping together." "Me!" said Charlie excitedly. "Me too!" said Alicia, echoed by others. "Yes, Charlie, and Alicia, and Mark went camping," acknowledged Joan, going on to name every child. "They put their sleeping bags in the car, and they put their tent in the car, and they put their food in the car. Then they put all themselves in the car, and they drove and drove until they got to the camping place." "In the mountains," explained Mark. "In the mountains," agreed Joan. "They got out of the car . . ." "I got out of the car," said Alicia. "Alicia got out of the car, and Paul got out of the car, and everybody got out of the car. They took their tent out of the car, and they put it up. They put their sleeping bags in the tent. They cooked their dinner." "On the fire," said Charlie. "They cooked their dinner on the fire and they ate it all up. They went to sleep in their sleeping bags. In the morning they got up and they cooked their breakfast and ate it all up . . . . And after they were all through camping, they put everything in the car, and they cleaned up every bit of their campsite, and that was the end."

Joan Newcomb, teaching at The Little School in Bellevue, Washington, is telling children a story about themselves in the same way that families do. In conversation she cites Newson and Newson's (1976) claim that storytelling about their children is one of the most important aspects of good parenting.

> The child is dependent on his parents' role as a memory bank to which he can continually refer for evidence of himself as an individual with a history. One of the means by which the ordinary child achieves a sense of personal identity is through his store of memories going back into his own past. . . . It must be remembered that the child does not maintain this store of memories on his own, but has them repaired, added to and embroidered upon in everyday conversation with his own family. (p. 404)

Looking back in her teaching, Joan remembers a home visit.

Everyone, including the siblings, had a humorous story to relate about the youngest child, Forrest, who was in my class. "Remember the time Forrest hid the peas from dinner in his diaper?" Forrest even joined in telling stories about himself. It was obviously a well-developed family sport. It gave me the feeling that this family had a special quality I can only describe as glueyness. (Newcomb, personal communication, 1990)

What is the "glue" that brings a family, or a class, together? Joan as story-teller is re-creating the play of the 3-year-olds, using her words to involve them in the making of a communal art form. The children have invented and played their version of the story; some of them were eager to retell it with her. Others listened. If they're interested, she'll tell it again on another day: "Remember when you all went camping?," inviting memory of past events and creating a shared tradition that builds group cohesion—a sense of the "we" who do memorable things together.

Joan also adds artifacts to some of her stories, introducing objects with which the children were playing: "And the last time anybody saw that ghost, she was wearing this exact same hood." Becoming a prop in a story elevates a familiar object to a new level, Joan says. It becomes in great demand in the play that follows.

Because these children are 3-year-olds, the teacher's retelling is oral, with liberal use of gestures and props. By the time they're 4 or 5, some of the children will also be interested in written words, which have their own sorts of rhythm on the page.

We all went camping.
Charlie went camping.
Alicia went camping.
Mark went camping.
Paul went camping.
We all went camping yesterday.

FROM HERE AND NOW TO THERE AND THEN: BUILDING BRIDGES OF MEANING

Oral and written retelling of children's play is an approach we described in Chapter 6. We have also given examples of teacher drawings of children's play activities and constructions–another mode of retelling, with images. Vivian Paley (1981) has invented still another approach to retelling: guided dramatization by children of their dictated stories.

All these approaches make a direct transition into language-experience and whole-language approaches to teaching literacy to older children. If Joan had in fact written the children's camping story, she would have had a language-experience chart (Van Allen, 1976; Veatch, Sawicki, Elliott, Barnette, & Blakey, 1973). The patterned language of memorable stories can not only be shared in storytelling but also discovered in Big Books (Holdaway, 1979). Children can "write" as well as dictate their stories, inventing writing for themselves in the process (Harris, 1988; Heigl, 1988). Children simultaneously talk, draw, and write their own stories (Dyson, 1989; Genishi & Dyson, 2009). Words that loom large in importance in children's play and stories can be written for them to copy and expand into written stories (Ashton-Warner, 1963; Clemens, 1983; Johnson, 1987). Curriculum themes introduced by the teacher can serve as an integrated focus within which all these activities can go on, building a shared classroom culture, just as John Dewey (1938, 1990/1943) proposed.

All these activities may begin in kindergarten or with 4-year-olds and be fully implemented in the primary grades. All build bridges of meaning for children. Both in preschool and in primary, the teacher sustains and participates in children's creative process by inventing conscious, sustained responses to their stories and images. Teachers represent the child's words and images back to the child in ways that both affirm the meanings and model different ways in which meanings can be represented.

With 3- to 5-year-olds it seems to us particularly important that teachers represent for children not only their dictated stories but their *play*. Play is what young children do best; in play, they are at their most thoughtful and articulate, using body language as well as words. To represent children's play, the teacher must pay attention to it, noting the scripts children are playing and selecting the content to be recorded. In contrast, when taking dictation from a child while other children are playing, the teacher is ignoring the play. It is important, we believe, to pay attention to play.

In the High/Scope preschool curriculum (High/Scope.org), children come together after play for *review*, at which they are asked to talk about their play. In the oversimplified version often adopted by teachers, review becomes a classification exercise. "Where did you play?" "I played in the block area." "Who did you play with?" "I played with Juanito." The richness of the playscripts, which included fantasy and feelings as well as mundane facts, is lost when young children are asked to talk, in a group, about the play they have already played.

Preschool teachers, Tizard and Hughes (1984) have found, ask children questions about their play—often questions to which they already know the answers, like those above. In contrast, the mothers in Tizard and Hughes's sample (both working-class and middle-class) discussed a wider range of topics with their children.

> At school, because the talk concerned play, it was almost always concerned with the "here and now." At home, events outside the present context, including the child's own past and future, were more often discussed. . . . The school curriculum was, in fact, considerably narrower than the home's—a smaller range of topics was discussed. (p. 183)

Adult-child conversations at school were briefer than those at home and much more adult-dominated. "It was the staff who tended to keep the conversation going, and who did most of the talking" (p. 186).

The question "Can you tell me about your play?," like the question "Can you tell me about your painting?," implies that meaning can be communicated only through words—that drama and art need prose explanation. It is, in fact, a teacher question, designed not to get real information but to stimulate oral language. Tizard and Hughes (1984) describe a conversation between a teacher and a child named Joyce; they then ask:

> Why are the teacher and child talking at all? Clearly it is not because Joyce has anything she wants to say to the teacher at this particular moment. Rather, the conversation is taking place because the teacher sees an opportunity to introduce certain educational ideas (in this case, to do with size

and shape) into the child's play. . . . Joyce does not respond with enthusiasm to this approach. (p. 191)

In a good home, children's play is not the focus of attention. In a good early childhood program, it is—because most of the people present are children and what they do together is play. The primary responsibility of the adults present is to facilitate play. But it is also their responsibility, we believe, to do what adults do much better than young children—to expand children's experience to include the there and then as well as the here and now.

Mothers and fathers in good homes ask questions to which they don't already know the answers, and they give information to children about matters of mutual interest (Tizard & Hughes, 1984). The parent-child relationship is a genuine and long-lasting one; information-giving thus includes stories about past and future events in the family's life. Quality early childhood programs take the family rather than the school as their model (Prescott, 1978). This implies both plenty of opportunities for informal adult-child conversations and, in the group, storytelling *by the adult* rather than review or show-and-tell by the children.

Adult storytelling comes from books and traditional tales. It comes from trips we've taken together and events we're planning for next week. And it can come from a teacher's observations of the children, using her skills to recapture the scripts from their play, inviting but not requiring their participation in the retelling. (Teachers familiar with the call-and-response tradition characteristic of storytelling in some cultures may find ways to involve children in story participation just as they do in action songs, but with responses developed by the group members to fit their own story. "In the mountains," said Mark. "On the fire," said Charlie.)

The spontaneous play of young children is their highest achievement. In their play, children invent the world for themselves and create a place for themselves in it. They are re-creating their pasts and imagining their futures while grounding themselves in the reality and fantasy of their lives here and now. Re-creating children's play in her own words, the teacher shows respect for its integrity, while building on it as one of the shared, recurrent experiences out of which the group's culture can grow. For this purpose, as well as for play's inherent value for children, teachers need to pay attention to play.

References

Alfieri, L., Brooks, P. J., Aldrich, N. J., & Tenenbaum, H. R. (2010). Does discovery-based instruction enhance learning? *Journal of Educational Psychology* [advance online publication]. doi: 10.1037/a0021017.

Ashton-Warner, S. (1963). *Teacher.* New York: Simon and Schuster.

Ballesteros, D. (1988). A language-enhancing classroom. In E. Jones (Ed.), *Reading, writing, and talking with four, five and six year olds* (pp. 129–135). Pasadena, CA: Pacific Oaks College.

Berk, L. (2006). *Child development* (7th ed.). Boston: Allyn & Bacon.

Bereiter, C., & Engelmann, S. (1966). *Teaching disadvantaged children in the preschool.* Englewood Cliffs, NJ: Prentice Hall.

Bissex, G. (1980). *GNYS at work: A child learns to write and read.* Cambridge, MA: Harvard University Press.

Bodrova, E., Leong, D., & Shore, R. (2004). Child outcome standards in pre-K programs: What are standards? What is needed to make them work? *National Institute for Early Education Research, 5,* 1–12.

Bredekamp, S. (Ed.). (1987). *Developmentally appropriate practice in early childhood programs serving children from birth to age 8.* Washington, DC: National Association for the Education of Young Children.

Bredekamp, S. (2004). Play and school readiness. In E. F. Zigler, D. G. Singer, & S. J. Bishop-Josef (Eds.), *Children's play: The roots of reading.* Washington, DC: Zero to Three Press.

Bredekamp, S., & Copple, C. (2009). *Developmentally appropriate practice in early childhood programs: Serving children from birth through age 8* (3rd ed.). Washington, DC: National Association for the Education of Young Children.

Brereton, A. E. (2010). Is teaching sign language in early childhood classrooms feasible for busy teachers and beneficial for children? *Young Children, 65*(4), 92–97.

Bronson, P., & Merryman, A. (2010). The creativity crisis. *Newsweek, 156*(3). Retrieved from http://www.newsweek.com/2010/07/10/the-creativity-crisis.html.

Brown, R. (2000). *Snail trail.* London: Andersen Press.

Campbell, F. A., Pungello, E. P., Miller-Johnson, S., Burchinal, M., & Ramey, C. T. (2001). The development of cognitive and academic abilities: Growth curves from an early childhood education experiment. *Developmental Psychology, 37,* 231–242.

Campbell, F. A., & Ramey, C. T. (1995). Cognitive and school outcomes for high-risk African-American students at middle adolescence: Positive effects of early intervention. *American Educational Research Journal, 32,* 743–772.

Campbell, F. A., Ramey, C. T., Pungello, E. P., Sparling, J., & Miller-Johnson, S. (2002). Early childhood education: Young adult outcomes from the Abecedarian Project. *Applied Developmental Science, 6,* 42–57.

Carlsson-Paige, N., & Levin, D. (2006). *The war play dilemma: What every parent and teacher needs to know* (2nd ed.). New York: Teachers College Press.

Carroll, L. (1979). *Alice's adventures in wonderland.* New York: Grosset & Dunlap. (Original work published 1865).

Carter, M. (2001, November). Rethinking our environments. *Child Care Information Exchange, 142,* 54–56.

Carter, M., & Jones, E. (1990). The teacher as observer: The director as role model. *Child Care Information Exchange, 75,* 27–30.

Chein, N., Howes, C., Burchinal, M., Painta, R., Ritchie, S., Bryant, D., et al. (2010). Children's classroom engagement and school readiness gains in prekindergarten. *Child Development, 81*(5), 1534–1550.

Clemens, S. G. (1983). *The sun's not broken, a cloud's just in the way.* Mt. Rainier, MD: Gryphon House.

Clements, D. H., & Sarama, J. (2009). *Learning and teaching early math: The learning trajectories approach.* London: Routledge.

Cochran-Smith, M., & Lytle, S. L. (2006). Troubling images of teaching in No Child Left Behind. *Harvard Educational Review, 76*(4), 668–697.

Cohen, R., Tunick, B. P., & Seaburg, K. (1993). *Snail trails and tadpole tails: Nature education for young children.* St. Paul, MN: Redleaf Press.

Coles, R. (1989). *The call of stories. Teaching and the moral imagination.* Boston: Houghton Mifflin.

Csikszentmihalyi, M. (1990). *Flow: The psychology of optimal experience.* New York: HarperCollins.

Curtis, D. (2010, July/August). Really seeing children: Seeing and supporting children's kinship with the natural world. *Exchange, 188,* 20–24.

Curtis, D., & Carter, M. (2008). *Learning together with young children: A curriculum framework for reflective teachers.* St. Paul, MN: Redleaf Press.

Delpit, L. (1986). Skills and other dilemmas of a progressive black educator. *Harvard Educational Review, 56*(4), 379–385.

Delpit, L. (1988). The silenced dialogue: Power and pedagogy in educating other people's children. *Harvard Educational Review, 58*(3), 280–298.

Derman-Sparks, L., & Ramsey, P.G. (2011). *What if all the kids are white?: Anti-bias multicultural education with young children and families* (2nd ed.). New York: Teachers College Press.

DeVries, R., & Kohlberg, L. (1990). *Constructivist early education: Overview and comparison with other programs.* Washington, DC: National Association for the Education of Young Children.

Dewey, J. (1938). *Experience and education.* New York: Macmillan.

Dewey, J. (1943). *The school and society.* New York: Macmillan. (Original work published 1900)

Diamond, A., Barnett, W. S., Thomas, J., & Munro, S. (2007). Preschool program improves cognitive control. *Science, 318,* 1387–1388

Dodge, D. T. (1993). Places for all children: Building environments for differing needs. *Child Care Information Exchange, 93,* 40–44.

Donaldson, M. (1978). *Children's minds.* Glasgow, Scotland: Fontana/Collins.

Donmoyer, R. (1981). The politics of play: Ideological and organizational constraints on the inclusion of play experiences in the school curriculum. *Journal of Research and Development in Education, 14*(3), 11–18.

Duckworth, E. (2007). *"The having of wonderful ideas" and other essays on teaching and learning* (3rd ed.). New York: Teachers College Press.

Duncan, G., Claessens, A., Huston, A., Pagani, L., Engel, M., Sexton, H., & Japel, C. (2007). School readiness and later achievement. *Developmental Psychology, 43*, 1428–1446.

Dyson, A. H. (1989). *Multiple worlds of child writers: Friends learning to write.* New York: Teachers College Press.

Early, D. M., Barbarin, O., Bryant, D. M., Burchinal, M., Chang, F., Clifford, R., M., & Weaver, W. (2005). Pre-kindergarten in eleven states: NCEDL's multistate study of pre-kindergarten and study of State-Wide Early Education Programs (SWEEP): Preliminary descriptive report. Retrieved from http://www.plan4preschool.org/docs/single/pre-kindergarten-in-eleven-states/

Eaton, M. (1997). Positive discipline: Fostering the self-esteem of young children. *Young Children, 52*(6), 43–46.

Edwards, C., Gandini, L., & Forman, G. (1998). *The hundred languages of children: The Reggio Emilia approach–Advanced reflections* (2nd ed.). Greenwich, CT: Ablex.

Egan, K. (1989*). Teaching as storytelling.* Chicago: University of Chicago Press.

Elkind, D. (1989, October). Developmentally appropriate practice: Philosophical and practical implications. *Phi Delta Kappan, 71*(2): 113–117.

Elkind, D. (2008a). Can we play? *Greater Good, 4,* 14–17.

Elkind, D. (2008b, March/April). Some misunderstandings of school readiness. *Exchange,* 49–52.

Epstein, A. S. (2009, January/February). Think before you (inter)act: What it means to be an intentional teacher. *Exchange, 179,* 46–49.

Erikson, E. (1950). *Childhood and society.* New York: Norton.

Ferreiro, E., & Teberosky, A. (1982). *Literacy before schooling.* Portsmouth, NH: Heinemann.

Fisher, K., Hirsh-Pasek, K., Golinkoff, R. M., Berk, L., & Singer, D. (2010). Playing around in school: Implications for learning and educational policy. In A. Pellegrini (Ed.), *The Oxford Handbook of the development of play.* New York: Oxford University Press.

Fisher, K., Hirsh-Pasek, K., Newcombe, N., & Golinkoff, R. M. (2011). When playful learning trumps direct instruction: The case of shape learning. In T. R. Westbrook & A. Gopnik (Chairs), *Playful learning: Pedagogy and policy.* Symposium conducted at the 2011 meeting of the Society for Research in Child Development, Montreal, Canada.

Forman, G. (1989). Helping children ask good questions. In B. Neugebauer (Ed.), *The wonder of it: Exploring how the world works* (pp. 21–24). Redmond, WA: Exchange Press.

Forman, G. (1996, March). Negotiating with art media to deepen learning. *Child Care Information Exchange, 108,* 56–58.

Forman, G., & Fyfe, B. (1998). Negotiated learning through design, documentation, and discourse. In C. Edwards, L. Gandini, & G. Forman (Eds.), *The hundred languages of children: The Reggio Emilia approach–Advanced reflections* (2nd ed., pp. 239–260). Greenwich, CT: Ablex.

Franklin, M., & Biber, B. (1977). Psychological perspectives and early childhood education: Some relations between theory and practice. In L. Katz (Ed.), *Current topics in early childhood education* (Vol. 1, pp. 1–32). Norwood, NJ: Ablex.

Freire, P. (1970). *Pedagogy of the oppressed.* New York: Seabury.

Fromberg, D. P. (2002). *Play and meaning in early childhood education.* Boston: Allyn & Bacon.

Genishi, C., & Dyson, A. H. (2009). *Children, language, and literacy: Diverse learners in diverse times.* New York: Teachers College Press.

Gonzalez-Mena, J., & Eyer, D. W. (1989). *Infants, toddlers, and caregivers.* Mountain View, CA: Mayfield.

Gonzalez-Mena, J., & Stonehouse, A. (2008). *Making links: A collaborative approach to planning and practice in early childhood programs.* New York: Teachers College Press.

Gopnik, A. (2009). *The philosophical baby: What children's minds tell us about truth, love, and the meaning of life.* New York: Farrar, Straus and Giroux.

Graves, D. (1983). *Writing: Teachers and children at work.* Portsmouth, NH: Heinemann.

Greenman, J. (1988). *Caring spaces, learning places: Children's environments that work.* Redmond, WA: Exchange Press.

Greer Jarman, C. (1999, January). The culture of play: A personal perspective. *Child Care Information Exchange, 125,* 52–54.

Griffin, E. F. (1982). *Island of childhood: Education in the special world of the nursery school.* New York: Teachers College Press.

Gronlund, G. (1992). Coping with Ninja Turtle play in my kindergarten classroom. *Young Children, 48*(1), 21–25.

Gronlund, G. (2006). *Make early learning standards come alive: Connecting your practice and curriculum to state standards.* St. Paul, MN: Redleaf Press; Washington, DC: National Association for the Education of Young Children.

Han, M., Moore, N., Vukelich, C., & Buell, M. (in press). Does play make a difference? Effects of play intervention on at-risk preschoolers' vocabulary learning. *American Journal of Play.*

Harris, L. (1988). Journal writing at Pine Hill. In E. Jones (Ed.), *Reading, writing and talking with four, five and six years olds* (pp. 207–219). Pasadena, CA: Pacific Oaks College.

Harste, J., Woodward, V., & Burke, C. (1984). *Language stories and literacy lessons.* Portsmouth, NH: Heinemann.

Hawkins, D. (2002). *The informed vision: Essays on learning and human nature.* New York: Algora Press.

Hawkins, F. P. (1974). *The logic of action.* New York: Pantheon Books.

Heath, S. B. (1983). *Ways with words: Language, life and work in communities and classrooms.* Cambridge, UK: Cambridge University Press.

Heigl, J. (1988). Language experiences for language-delayed children. In E. Jones (Ed.), *Reading, writing and talking with four, five and six year olds* (pp. 121–128). Pasadena, CA: Pacific Oaks College.

Helm, J. H. (2008). Got standards? Don't give up on engaged learning. *Young Children, 63*(4), 14–20.

Helm, J. H., & Katz, L. (2010). *Young investigators: The project approach in the early years* (2nd ed.). New York: Teachers College Press.

Hirsh-Pasek, K., Golinkoff, R. M., Berk, L. E., & Singer, D. G. (2009). *A mandate for playful learning in the preschool: Presenting the evidence.* New York: Oxford University Press.

Hohmann, M., Banet, B., & Weikart, D. P. (1979). *Young children in action: A manual for preschool educators.* Ypsilanti, MI: High/Scope.

Holdaway, D. (1979). *The foundations of literacy.* Portsmouth, NH: Heinemann.

Howarth, M. (1988). Fairy tale dramatics: An approach to oral language and personal meaning. In E. Jones (Ed.), *Reading, writing and talking with four, five and six year olds* (pp. 159–173). Pasadena, CA: Pacific Oaks College.

Howarth, M. (1989). Rediscovering the power of fairy tales: They help children understand their lives. *Young Children, 45*(1), 58–65.

Johnson, K. (1987). *Doing words.* Boston: Houghton Mifflin.

Jones, E. (1983). On the use of behavioral objectives in open education. In E. Jones (Ed.), *On the growing edge: Notes by college teachers making changes* (pp. 63–66). Pasadena, CA: Pacific Oaks College.

Jones, E. (1984). Training individuals: In the classroom and out. In J. T. Greenman & R. W. Fuqua (Eds.), *Making day care better: Training, evaluation, and the process of change* (pp. 185–201). New York: Teachers College Press.

Jones, E., & Cooper, R. M. (2006). *Playing to get smart.* New York: Teachers College Press.

Jones, E., & Meade-Roberts, J. (1991). *Assessment through observation: A profile of developmental outcomes* [occasional paper]. Pacific Oaks College, Pasadena, CA.

Jones, E., & Nimmo, J. (1994). *Emergent curriculum.* Washington, DC: National Association for the Education of Young Children.

Jones, E., & Prescott, E. (1982). Day care: Short- or long-term solution? In W. M. Bridgeland & E. A. Duane (special eds.), *Young Children and Social Policy* [The Annals of the American Academy of Political and Social Science, Vol. 461, May 1982, pp. 91–101].

Kamii, C. (1985). Leading primary education toward excellence: Beyond worksheets and drill. *Young Children, 40*(6), 3–9.

Kamii, C. (2000). *Young children reinvent arithmetic: Implications of Piaget's theory* (2nd ed.). New York: Teachers College Press.

Katz, L. G. (1980). Mothering and teaching: Some significant distinctions. In L. Katz et al. (Eds.), *Current topics in early childhood education: Vol. III* (pp. 47–63). Norwood, NJ: Ablex.

Katz, L. G. (2008, March/April). Another look at what young children should be learning. *Exchange, 174,* 53–56.

Katz, L. G., & Chard, S. (2000). *Engaging children's minds: The project approach* (2nd ed.). Norwood, NJ: Ablex.

Keeler, R. (2008, November/December). A natural playscape: Four years later. *Exchange, 178,* 84–85.

Kipling, R. (1978). *Just so stories.* New York: Weathervane Books. (Original work published 1902)

Kritchevsky, S., & Prescott, E. (1969). *Planning environments for young children: Physical space.* Washington, DC: National Association for the Education of Young Children.

Kuschner, D. (1989). Put your name on your painting but . . . the blocks go back on the shelves. *Young Children, 45*(1), 45–56.

Leong, D. J., & Bodrova, E. (2009, October). *Developing self-regulation by developing intentional make believe play.* Paper presented at the School Readiness Conference in Quebec City, Canada.

Levin, D. E. (2008, September/October). Building peaceable communities: Counteracting the impact of violence on young children. *Exchange, 180,* 57–60.

Levin, D. E. (2009, May/June). Too young to be a consumer: The toll of commercial culture on the rights of childhood. *Exchange, 181,* 49–52.

Lewin-Benham, A. (2010). *Infants & toddlers at work: Using Reggio-inspired materials to support brain development.* New York: Teachers College Press.

Li-Grining, C., Votruba-Drzal, E., Maldonado-Carreno, C., & Haas, K. (2010). Children's early approaches to learning and academic trajectories through fifth grade. *Developmental Psychology, 46,* 1062–1078.

Maslow, A. (1962). *Toward a psychology of being.* New York: Van Nostrand Reinhold.

McLeod, E. W. (1961). *One snail and me.* Boston: Little Brown.

Meade-Roberts, J. (1988). It's all academic! In E. Jones (Ed.), *Reading, writing and talking with four, five and six year olds* (pp. 91–103). Pasadena, CA: Pacific Oaks College.

Meier, T., & Murrell, P. (1996). "They can't even play right!": Cultural myopia in the analysis of play–Cultural perspectives on human development. In A. L. Phillips (Ed.), *Topics in early childhood education: Vol. 2. Playing for keeps: Supporting children's play* (pp. 99–113). St. Paul, MN: Redleaf Press.

Miller, E., & Almon, J. (2009). *Crisis in the kindergarten: Why children need to play in school.* College Park, MD: Alliance for Childhood.

Miller, J. B. (1976). *Toward a new psychology of women.* Boston: Beacon Press.

Monighan-Nourot, P. (1990). The legacy of play in American early childhood education. In E. Klugman & S. Smilansky (Eds.), *Children's play and learning* (pp. 59–85). New York: Teachers College Press.

National Association for the Education of Young Children. (1994). *Media violence in children's lives.* Washington, DC: Author.

National Association for the Education of Young Children. (2003). *Early childhood curriculum, assessment, and program evaluation: Building an effective, accountable system in programs for children birth through age 8.* Washington, DC: Author.

National Association for the Education of Young Children. (2009). *Developmentally appropriate practice in early childhood programs serving children from birth through age 8.* Washington, DC: Author.

New, R. (1990). Excellent early education: A city in Italy has it. *Young Children, 45*(6), 4–10.

Newson, J., & Newson, E. (1976). *Seven years old in the home environment.* London: Allen and Unwin.

Nicholson, S. (1974). How not to cheat children: The theory of loose parts. In G. Coates (Ed.), *Alternate learning environments.* Stroudsberg, PA: Dowden, Hutchinson, and Ross.

Noddings, N. (2003). *Caring: A feminine approach to ethics and moral education* (2nd ed). Berkeley: University of California Press.

Paley, V. G. (1981). *Wally's stories.* Cambridge, MA: Harvard University Press.

Paley, V. G. (1984). *Boys and girls: Superheroes in the doll corner.* Chicago: University of Chicago Press.

Paley, V. G. (1986a). *Mollie is three: Growing up in school.* Chicago: University of Chicago Press.

Paley, V G. (1986b). On listening to what the children say. *Harvard Educational Review, 56*(2), 122–131.

Paley, V, G. (1988). *Bad guys don't have birthdays: Fantasy play at four.* Chicago: University of Chicago Press.

Paley, V. G. (1990). *The boy who would be a helicopter: The uses of storytelling in the classroom.* Cambridge, MA: Harvard University Press.

Paley, V. G. (2004). *A child's work: The importance of fantasy play.* Chicago: University of Chicago Press.

Paley, V. G. (2009). Afterword. In E. Miller & J. Almon, *Crisis in the kindergarten: Why children need to play in school* (p. 61). College Park, MD: Alliance for Childhood.

Peters, E. (1996). Aboriginal people in urban areas. In D. A. Long & O. P. Dickason (Eds.), *Visions of the heart: Canadian aboriginal issues* (pp. 305–333). Toronto, ON: Harcourt Brace.

Peterson, R., & Felton-Collins, V. (1986). *The Piaget handbook for teachers and parents.* New York: Teachers College Press.

Piaget, J. (1962). *Play, dreams and imitation in childhood.* New York: Norton.

Piaget, J. (1973). *To understand is to invent.* New York: Grossman.

Prescott, E. (1978). Is day care as good as a good home? *Young Children, 33*(2), 13–19.

Prescott, E., Jones, E., Kritchevsky, S., Milich, C., & Haselhoef, E. (1975). *Who thrives in group day care?* Pasadena, CA: Pacific Oaks College.

Rabiroff, B., & Prescott, E. (1978). The invisible child: Challenge to teacher attentiveness. In E. Jones (Ed.), *Joys and risks in teaching young children* (pp. 123–133). Pasadena, CA: Pacific Oaks College.

Reynolds, A., Ou, S., & Topitzes, J. W. (2004). Paths of effects of early childhood intervention on educational attainment and delinquency: A confirmatory analysis of the Chicago Child-Parent Centers. *Child Development, 75,* 1299–1328.

Reynolds, G. (1988). When I was little I used to play a lot. In E. Jones (Ed.), *Reading, writing and talking with four, five and six year olds* (pp. 85–90). Pasadena, CA: Pacific Oaks College.

Reynolds, G. (1998). Reggio Emilia—An impossible dream? *Canadian Children: Journal of the Canadian Association for Young Children, 23*(2), 4–10.

Reynolds, G. (2002). The welcoming place: Tungasuvvingat Inuit Head Start program. In C. R. Brown & C. Marchant (Eds.), *Play in practice: Case studies in young children's play* (pp. 87–104). St. Paul, MN: Redleaf.

Reynolds, G., & Jones, E. (1997). *Master players: Learning from children at play.* New York: Teachers College Press.

Rinaldi, C. (2006). *In dialogue with Reggio Emilia: Listening, researching, and learning.* London: Routledge.

Rochman, B. (2011, March). In preschool, what matters more: Education or play? *Time Healthland.* Retrieved from http://healthland.time.com/2011/03/23/playing-at-preschool-mom-says-no-way/

Rogoff, B. (2003). *The cultural nature of human development.* New York: Oxford University Press.

Salazar, R., & Schulze, M. C. (2010). *Modelando con niños menores de seis anos (Modeling with children under six years old)*. Available at www.worldforumfoundation.org

Sarama, J., & Clements, D. H. (2009, Winter). Building blocks and cognitive building blocks: Playing to know the world mathematically. *American Journal of Play, 2*(3), 13–337.

Schweinhart, L. J. (2004). *The High/Scope Perry preschool study through age 40: Summary, conclusions, and frequently asked questions.* Ypsilanti, MI: High/Scope Educational Research Foundation.

Segal, M., & Adcock, D. (1981). *Just pretending: Ways to help children grow through imaginative play.* Englewood Cliffs, NJ: Prentice Hall.

Sendak, M. (1962). *Pierre.* New York: Harper & Row.

Singer, D. G., Golinkoff, R. M., & Hirsh-Pasek, K. (Eds.). (2006). *Play = learning: How play motivates and enhances children's cognitive and social-emotional growth.* New York: Oxofrd University Press.

Slobodkina, E. (1947). *Caps for sale.* New York: Scott.

Smilansky, S. (1968). *The effects of sociodramatic play on disadvantaged preschool children.* New York: Wiley.

Smilansky, S., & Shefatya, L. (1990). *Facilitating play: A medium for promoting cognitive, socioemotional and academic development in young children.* Gaithersburg, MD: Psychosocial and Educational Publications.

Snow, C. E. (1983). Literacy and language: Relationships during the preschool years. *Harvard Educational Review, 53*(2), 185–189.

Solow, J. (1989). *Words through wonder.* Unpublished master's thesis, Pacific Oaks College, Pasadena, CA.

Sparrow, B. (1988). What really matters: The teacher in the concentrated encounter. In E. Jones (Ed.), *Reading, writing, and talking with four, five, and six year olds* (pp. 232–240). Pasadena, CA: Pacific Oaks College.

Stacey, S. (2009). *Emergent curriculum in early childhood settings: From theory to practice.* St. Paul, MN: Redleaf Press.

Stadler, S. (1990). *Layers of learning: Literacy for children and teachers.* Unpublished master's thesis, Pacific Oaks College, Pasadena, CA.

Stallibrass, A. (1989). *The self-respecting child: A study of children's play and development.* Reading, MA: Addison-Wesley.

Stritzel, K. (1989). *Blockbuilding and gender.* Unpublished master's thesis, Pacific Oaks College, Pasadena, CA.

Sulzby, E. (1986). Signs of oral and written language organization in the young child. In W. H. Teale & E. Sulzby (Eds.), *Emergent literacy: Writing and reading* (pp. 50–89). Norwood, NJ: Ablex.

Suransky, V. P. (1982). *The erosion of childhood.* Chicago: University of Chicago Press.

Sutton-Smith, B. (1997). *The ambiguity of play.* Cambridge, MA: Harvard University Press.

Tizard, B., & Hughes, M. (1984). *Young children learning: Talking and thinking at home and at school.* London: Fontana/Collins.

Toffler, A. (1980). *The third wave.* New York: Morrow.

Topal, C. W., & Gandini, L. (1999). *Beautiful stuff! Learning with found materials.* Worcester, MA: Davis.

Trook, E. (1983). Understanding teachers' use of power: A role-playing activity. In E. Jones (Ed.), *On the growing edge: Notes by college teachers making changes* (pp. 15–22). Pasadena, CA: Pacific Oaks College.

Van Allen, R. (1976). *Language experiences in communication.* Boston: Houghton Mifflin.

Van Hoorn, J., Nourot, P. M., Scales, B., & Alward, K. A. (2011). *Play at the center of the curriculum* (5th ed.). Upper Saddle River, NJ: Pearson.

Veatch, J., Sawicki, F., Elliott, G., Barnette, E., & Blakey, J. (1973). *Key words to reading: The language experience approach begins.* Columbus, OH: Merrill.

Vygotsky, L. S. (1978). *Mind in society: The development of higher psychological processes.* Cambridge, MA: Harvard University Press.

Wassermann, S. (2000). *Serious players in the primary classroom: Empowering children through active learning experiences* (2nd ed.). New York: Teachers College Press.

Watzlawick, P., Weakland, J., & Fisch, R. (1974). *Change: Principles of problem formation and problem resolution.* New York: Norton.

Weikart, D. P. (1998). Changing early childhood development through educational intervention. *Preventive Medicine, 27,* 233–237.

Wien, C. A. (Ed.). (2008). *Emergent curriculum in the primary classroom: Interpreting the Reggio Emilia approach in schools.* New York: Teachers College Press.

Wien, C. A. (1994). *Developmentally appropriate practice in "real life"–Stories of teacher practical knowledge.* New York: Teachers College Press.

Wien, C. A., & Kirby-Smith, S. (1998). Untiming the curriculum: A case study of removing clocks from the program. *Young Children 53*(5), 8–13.

Wing, L. A. (1995). Play is not the work of the child. *Early Childhood Research Quarterly, 10*(2), 223–247.

Zigler, E., Singer, D., & Bishop-Josef, S. (Eds.). (2004). *Children's play: The roots of reading.* Washington, DC: Zero to Three Press.

Index

About the Authors

Elizabeth Jones is faculty emerita in Human Development at Pacific Oaks College in Pasadena, California, where she has also taught in the preschool and primary children's programs. She earned an M.A. in Child Development at the University of Wisconsin and a Ph.D. in Sociology at the University of Southern California. She has been a visiting lecturer at the University of Alaska and was DeLissa Fellow at the South Australian College of Advanced Education, Adelaide, South Australia. She has consulted and presented at conferences around the world, as well as in Pasadena. Her books, published by Teachers College Press and by the National Association for the Education of Young Children (NAEYC), include *Master Players* (with Gretchen Reynolds), *Playing to Get Smart* (with Renatta Cooper), *Emergent Curriculum* (with John Nimmo), *The Lively Kindergarten* (with Kathleen Evans and Kay Rencken), *Teaching Adults,* and *Teaching Adults Revisited.*

Gretchen Reynolds is co-author, with Elizabeth Jones, of *Master Players: Learning from Children at Play* (Teachers College Press, 1997). She joined the faculty in the Early Childhood Education Program at Algonquin College (Ottawa, Canada) in 1992. Gretchen has presented at conferences and written numerous articles on giving value to children's play within community and in early learning programs. She participated in a Canadian International Development Agency project with the Egyptian Department of Education to train kindergarten teachers in early childhood curriculum. She collaborated with the Ottawa Inuit Children's Centre on culturally meaningful learning contexts for children and adults. Gretchen traveled with Canadians on study tours to schools in Reggio Emilia, Italy, and served on the board of the Ontario Reggio Association. She received an M.S. in Education from the Bank Street College of Education, New York City, and a Ph.D. in Education from the Claremont Graduate University, Claremont, CA.